Homestay

A Japanese Girl's Romantic ESL
Adventure in Vancouver, Canada

By GENE SKELLIG

www.fleacircusbooks.com

Publishing & marketing provided by Flea Circus Books.
"Flea Circus" is a registered trade mark.

DEDICATION

This book is dedicated to my former English students in the Osaka – Kyoto region of Japan, and to Overseas Training Center (OTC), my former employer (1996-1997).

Thanks also to the Vancouver Mokuyokai Society http://www.mokuyokai.bc.ca/index.html

ACKNOWLEDGMENTS

Thanks go to my wife, Irina, for giving me time to write; to my editors, Alan, in Japan and Glenn, in Canada. Special thanks to my sister-in-law for introducing me to Japanese culture and to her family for helping me out when I set out to work in Japan so many years ago.

DISCLAIMER

FORWARD

Homestay is intended for ESL students preparing for a trip to North America. It is written in natural English which will be extremely challenging for most students. However, by working through the vocabulary, idioms, slang and cultural information woven into this story the reader may elevate their English and their motivation to an entirely new level before their trip. Additional resources such as vocabulary-building activities, journal entries and discussion topics are provided for use with a conversational English partner. Go to: www.homestay-adventure-vancouver.blogspot.com for more. There you will also find useful links related to visiting Vancouver, British Columbia, Canada. This could lead to a real adventure for you if you are as dedicated, curious and adventurous as Sumiko Kichida!

TO TEACHERS

Assign *Homestay* (paperback or eBook) as homework for your ESL homestay prep course. The above blogsite may be of use. Deep discounts for bulk orders. To place an order, contact support@fleacircusbooks.com

ISBN: 0986883182
ISBN-13: 978-0-9868831-8-7

CONTENTS

Final note to Teacher and ESL Student:

While working your way through this novel, the student should use a highlighter to mark the book up (paperback) or write down in a notebook (eBook/Paperback) whenever a word, expression or other aspect of the story is confusing. Bring this up in your conversational English class or ask a natural English speaker to explain.

Keeping a simple journal of your thoughts about Sumiko's adventure, one chapter at a time, will enhance the effectiveness of this book as a learning vehicle.

Gene Skellig

PROLOGUE

WEDDING CRASHER

Sharon Donnelly was extremely nervous. She had crashed weddings before; but this time, it would be different.

The venue, Brock House, was one of the most beautiful and historic old houses in the city. Sandwiched between the sprawling forest and fields of Jericho Beach Park and the Royal Vancouver Yacht Club, Brock House was a heritage building on the waterfront of Vancouver's west side. One hundred years old, it was a Tudor-style estate with high ceilings, elegantly appointed rooms adorned with beautiful woodworking and a large, well-maintained lawn leading to a one-hundred meter wide stretch of sandy beach overlooking Burrard Inlet. Simply breathtaking, Brock House was one of her favorite locations for a wedding.

That's why sneaking into this one had such a special meaning for her. But as she made her way into the foyer of the estate she noticed that most of the real guests were Japanese. Sharon stuck out like a sore thumb.

Then she saw him and the world around her faded away. As the man approached her, Sharon was disarmed by his handsome face and by his blue eyes that seemed to gaze directly into her soul. But it was his ear-to-ear grin that made Sharon forget her worries and she felt safe in the warmth of his gaze. He seemed out of place; in a gathering of well-dressed people, this man wore a checkered shirt and rugged blue jeans. It did not matter that she could be found out at any minute and thrown out of the wedding reception. Just to be looked at by those welcoming eyes made her feel at ease.

"Hi there! You look lost," the man said, as he ushered Sharon out of the entry way and over to one side of the entrance. "What's your name?"

"Sharon Donnelly, what's yours?"

"I'm Derek Osborne. Believe it or not, I'm supposed to be the best man, and look at me, I'm still in my blue-jeans!"

"So you are with...?" Sharon tried her old trick of fishing for information so that she could quickly get a handle on the 'who's who' at the wedding. Usually, once she knew a few names, she could bluff her way through the small talk that always takes place at wedding parties.

"I'm with Chris, the Groom. I haven't even met the bride yet."

"Really? How is that possible?" she asked, hoping to pry some useful information out of Derek.

"I've been studying abroad for the past year and only got back home two days ago. But Chris kept me up to date on his romance. He even sent me some pictures of his lovely bride, so at least I'll recognize her when they arrive. So who are you with?"

Suddenly afraid now that the conversation had come around to her, Sharon tried to change the topic. "Er, I'm sort of friends of friends of theirs. John invited me. Have you seen him around?" Sharon used the name "John"—it was such a common name there was sure to be someone there with that name. She was hoping to misdirect Derek and change the subject.

"Sure, I think he's out on the stairs to the lawn. Why don't you head out that way? I've got to go and change into my tux. See you around?" he said, smiling at Sharon as he began heading up the stairs.

"Yeah, sure. It was nice to meet you, Derek".

As Sharon walked through the grand foyer of the old building she felt much more at ease. She had passed the first test - making other guests believe that she belonged. Now all she had to do was figure out where she would sit for the speeches and dinner. As she walked through the dining room she kept her eye open for a seating plan or the tell-tale signs of a table with unassigned place settings.

She could feel the hard marble floor through her high-heeled shoes as she walked. She smiled at the idea that, if everything went well, she could be dancing on that very floor in a few hours—maybe even with that handsome Derek Osborne.

She found the seating plan posted on a billboard off to one side of the room. When she began reading the names it became clear to her how things were organized. Five round tables were arranged much like the Olympic rings, one row of three in the back and one row of two in front.

There were a few other tables farther back, in the corners of the room. At the very front of there was one long table for the bride and groom, the parents of both and presumably the best man, Derek, that charming man whom she had just met, and—she sighed at this—his girlfriend or wife. Sharon was surprised at herself for feeling jealousy over a man she had just met.

As she read the names along the head table, Sharon saw that many of the names were written in beautiful artwork that she assumed must be Japanese. Each of these names was made of two pairs of two pictures each, drawn by hand in some type of black ink. She had no idea what they meant, but she was pretty sure that they were the names of the guests.

Sharon noticed that in many cases the second pair was the same as for other guests. In these names, the first character looked like a plus sign sitting on a plate which in turn was sitting on a box. The second one looked like a four-pane window, or perhaps—box made up of four small squares.

When she read the English names she saw that the one in the center of the head table was "Christopher McGee". A quick glance at the names revealed that there were many McGees in attendance. So that's the groom's family—good to know, she thought. And Sharon was in luck, there was a guest named 'John': Mr. John Clarke. That must be the 'John' whom Derek had referred to when Sharon said that she was "with John".

Sharon got back to looking at the names at the head table, trying to figure out who was with Derek. As far as the English names went, there seemed to be only one female and two males at the head table and the female had the same last name as the other male. So maybe, Sharon hoped, Derek was unattached.

After a few more minutes of studying the seating plan Sharon had decided which table to sit at. The table farthest from the head table had a few vacancies and seemed to have a group of children from Clan McGee. The only exception was Mr. and Mrs. John Clarke. Sharon found a blank slip of paper and a pen in the gutter of the bulletin-board and then hand-wrote her name on the slip. Now she really was 'with John'.

With the push of a pin she had assigned herself a seat at the back table. Now she had a plan! She also wrote her name, Sharon Donnelly, on a blank nametag and placed it on the table next to Mrs.

Andrea Clarke. There was ample space between Mrs. Clarke's plate and that of the next guest to slip in one more person, but there was no extra place setting there yet. The table had only been set for six. All of the other tables were set for eight guests so Sharon reasoned that was the overflow table where last-minute guests could be added— even the uninvited kind.

All she would have to do was complain to one of the handsome young waiters that her place setting was missing. They would quickly get her plates, cutlery and various types of glasses. She saw that there were four different sizes of crystal glasses. At least one must be for wine, another tall slender one for Champagne, another for perhaps a dessert liqueur, and yet another for what—water?

When she thought about the glasses Sharon looked at the small forest of wine bottles set out in the middle of the table, surrounding the beautiful flower arrangement. There were bottles of red wine, white wine and even a few rose-colored wines. Sharon noticed that most of the bottles had similar labels. The labels caught her eye because each had a sketch of a beautiful vineyard estate.

The sketch brought to mind her own dream of one day taking a tour of a vineyard. Each bottle also had a small embossed symbol printed in gold and silver, with some writing in the middle making a circle around a tiny purple flower which she recognized as a thistle in bloom.

She picked up a bottle of red wine and then noticed that the bottle had one difference from all the others. It had won some sort of "Gold Medal Prize" in a regional wine tasting contest. She read that the bottle was from the Barossa Valley in South Australia.

Her reading of the bottle was interrupted when some guests walked past her, so she put the bottle down and headed out in the same direction as other guests, towards the back exit from the dining hall.

Feeling much more confident, Sharon headed out through the French doors at the rear of the dining room. They opened onto a beautiful stone patio overlooking a sun-drenched lawn with the ocean just beyond. Guests were starting to take their seats on either side of the aisle. Elegant white chairs were laid out in two large groups, left and right, all facing the simple podium decorated with flowers.

So that's where the wedding will take place, Sharon thought as she accepted a glass of Champagne from a waiter. The Champagne was cool as it slid down her throat. She delighted at the tickly bubbliness of her favorite drink.

Her love for Champagne and formal events was probably at the root of her dangerous hobby of showing up uninvited to weddings. So far, having crashed at least a dozen weddings over the years, she had never been caught in the act. Each one of these capers was a real thrill and with any luck, tonight would be one of the best.

Four hours later, walking barefoot in the grass, Sharon had had a few too many glasses of Champagne. When she reached the stone bench at the far side of the garden, Derek was still there.

"I'm back," she said. "Now, we're all alone. You've got ten minutes to tell me all about how that wonderful couple I met. I want to know all about that homestay adventure that Sumiko spoke about in her speech!"

"Alright, Sharon, here it is." Derek began to recount the improbable story of Sumiko Kichida and her homestay adventure. Sharon listened as intently as a child being read a bedtime story. When Sharon seemed to fade, leaning into

Derek's shoulder as if falling asleep, Derek would soften his voice and then try to stop talking. Each time he did this, Sharon opened her eyes and insisted that he go on. As Derek spoke, Sharon began to fall asleep. With her eyes closed and with Derek's arm draped around her shoulders Sharon felt like she was wrapped up in a warm blanket, experiencing a beautiful dream.

A romantic and adventurous dream.

1

A HEAVY HEART

Sumiko was so deep in thought that she almost missed her stop on the Karasuma Line. As it was, she barely got off the subway at the Imadegawa Station before the doors closed behind her and the train accelerated down the track for Kuramaguchi Station.

Normally she would have gotten off the subway at Marutamachi Station so that she could take a long walk through Kyoto Gyoen, the Imperial Palace Garden in the center of Kyoto. After a full day of lectures she liked to spend an hour or so sitting on a park bench going over her school work before going home. Her habit of staying on top of her assignments and getting some of the reading done while the lectures were still fresh in her mind, had helped her in the furious competition for grades at Kyoto University. She needed top grades in her undergraduate studies if she had any hope of being admitted to Graduate School at Kyoto University's Research Center for Environmental Quality Management. With so many well qualified engineering graduates applying for the prestigious program, Sumiko had been constantly aware of the intense competition she was up against.

The long walk along Mushanokoji Dori to her family home on Kuromon Dori was her time to integrate her thoughts and prepare for at least three hours of study at home. But all of that was in the past now. She no longer had any need for such disciplined time management.

Today, with her final exams behind her, Sumiko had absolutely no homework. She felt hollow, as though some of the meaning in her life had left her. Her friends had tried to cheer her up by inviting her to go out to their favorite karaoke bar over on Marutamachi Dori, in Sakyo-ku, but she had declined. Somehow going out and getting drunk, staying up all night dancing and having fun, did not appeal to her. She had more serious things to think about.

The first was a problem she had worried about for the past several months. As her studies drew to a close, ending five years of continuous effort, Sumiko knew that she faced a major fork in the road.

The problem was: what was she to do with the rest of her life? At twenty-three years old, Sumiko knew what she did with her next couple of years would determine the rest of her life. She had discussed her choices time after time with her parents and always came to the same conclusion. There are only three choices for a young woman in Japan. She likened her choices to the three main choices at her favorite restaurant, where she and her classmates usually went, Café Independants, in the basement under Kyoto City Hall.

The first choice was the 'A-Set-O' life, where you get married to a man with good career prospects, support and encourage his success, and raise one or two children. This was the traditional life that her mother, Atsuko, wanted for her oldest daughter. Atsuko Kichida wanted grandchildren, she wanted to be Obaasan, a grandmother, and Sumiko knew it. But unlike many traditional Japanese mothers, Atsuko was a very tender and expressive mother. She and Sumiko were very close. Sumiko felt that she could trust her mother with any secret, joy, or fear in her life. So despite her own wishes, Sumiko's mother knew that the A-Set-O life was not for her adventurous and confident daughter.

Then there was the 'B-Set-O' life, where Sumiko would devote her life to her career as a chemical engineer specializing in high-temperature ceramic design. She would wind up working for Kyoto Ceramics, 'Kyocera', like her father. In that scenario, Sumiko would never have children. She would be married to the company and would ultimately end up a dried up and bitter old prune like her aunt, Honoko.

While there was some appeal in a lifetime of achievement and financial security that goes with a successful career, Sumiko loved children and hoped to have at least two or three one day. Truth be told, Sumiko thought to herself, even four children would be fun. All that crying, screaming, chaos, mess and theatrics somehow had a deep appeal to her. Of course such a large family would be highly unusual in Japan. In fact, Sumiko could not think of even one example of such a large family anywhere in Kyoto's Kamigyo Ward, where she grew up.

Finally, there was the 'C-Set-O' life, where she would not devote herself fully to her career, not marry well, and waste her best years having meaningless fun with her friends. Perhaps even some meaningless sex with the occasional 'bad boy' who catches her eye. The lifestyle of someone who has little respect for herself, other than to seek, and at times become, entertainment.

In this third lifestyle, she knew, she would have to work very hard in some type of no-where job. She would never have enough money to see the world and she would be financially dependant on her parents for the rest of her life.

To Sumiko, all three choices faced by young Japanese women were equally unacceptable. So she had made up her mind to take the fourth option, the road less traveled.

But how would she break the news to her father? After all that he had done for her, putting her though university, getting her those summer jobs at Kyocera, grooming her for entry into one of the best companies in the city? And how could she disappoint him by revealing that she was going to leave Japan - maybe never to return!

To Sumiko the worst part of it was breaking her father's heart. He had always been so supportive of her, providing her with everything she had ever asked for. Even now, with the economic crises in Japan making everything more difficult for the Kichida family, her father continued to pay for perks like her cell-phone, I-Pad, eBook reader and her own dedicated high-speed internet connection.

When she needed money to buy new clothes or go out with friends he would hand over a few Ichi man en notes without making a face. On top of all of that, her parents insisted that she take a vacation each and every year during her last four years at school. Sumiko was so engrossed in her studies that even though she did take short summer vacations she invariably squirreled away a few thousand dollars out of the annual vacation allowance. The $24,000 USD Sumiko had accumulated through a lifetime of careful savings would soon be spent, as long as she had the courage to follow through on her dream.

So it was with a heavy heart that Sumiko made her way home. As she crossed Horikawa Dori and walked the final half-kilometer to her home on Kuromon Dori, all of the familiar sights suddenly seemed alien to her.

The apartment buildings seemed to be much closer together than they should be, bearing down on her like an avalanche of stones. The roads seemed too narrow, with cars crammed into tiny concrete garages or parked tight to the cement fences and the sides of houses. The beer vending machines clustered on either side of the sento closest to her parents home now seemed ridiculous. Why do Japanese men need to drink a liter of beer after spending two hours washing and soaking in the hot waters of a sento anyhow? She had to admit, however, having a few sips of beer on the way home with the 'sento glow' radiating off of her totally relaxed and heated body could really feel nice at times.

As she continued the final few paces home, sudsy grey water began slushing out of a sewer pipe into an open grey-water trench along the side of the road. Her neighbors, the Yamada's, were doing their evening load of laundry. As the smell of the dirty water reached her and the damp humidity of the air wafted into her face, Sumiko felt as if her hair, her clothes and even her lungs were being filled with a disgusting backwash of another person's grimy, sweaty day. It almost made her choke.

The only antidote to the overly crowded and polluted way of life in urban Japan was to think of another place, somewhere over the rainbow as she liked to imagine, where the air was fresh and clean, the water in the streams was clear and drinkable and the sky was fully of fluffy white clouds floating across an open, forested, terrain.

Transported to a better place in her mind, she took in a fresh, invigorating breath of her imagined landscape, her decision once again certain. She stepped into the genkan of the Kichida family home, took off her shoes and kicked her slippers together so that she could slide her feet into them. As she did this, she thought to herself that the right thing to do was to spill her guts and get it off of her chest.

Her heart raced as she saw her father coming down into the genkan from inside the house.

"Oto-Sama, I am going to live in Canada." Sumiko said suddenly, without any preamble.

She had not even finished taking her shoes off, nor had she put on her slippers and taken even one step into the home. She just stood there in the genkan with her father.

Sumiko saw that he had his bathing kit and towel with him, preparing to head out to the sento for a bath and, of course, a beer afterwards. But rather than shock or anger on his face after hearing what his daughter had just blurted out, he smiled warmly at her.

"Sumichan, my little squirrel, do you have any idea how long I've waited to hear you say that?"

Sumiko was dumbstruck. "You mean you are not upset? How long have you known?"

"I have known longer than you, my child."

"What do you mean? Did Mama tell you?"

"Not at all. From the moment we all watched that movie together, back when you were about twelve years old, I knew that you were building a dream in your imagination. The lifestyle you saw in that movie, about that water bomber pilot who becomes a ghost, that was the start of it all. After that, you seemed to gravitate to every movie set in the wild west of North America. That, and your collection of travel magazines, homestay pamphlets and movie posters up on your bedroom wall made a pretty clear picture to me.

You would not be satisfied with a lifetime of diligent effort at Kyocera. And you are too enterprising to waste your life having fun like some of your friends. No, Sumichan, it has been in the cards for years that you would flee this smelly little birdcage we call our home, as soon as you finished university."

The contented look on her father's face made her cry. He loved her so much that even if it meant losing her he was willing to open the door of her very comfortable life, her gilded cage, and let her fly off on a risky adventure to a distant land.

With tears in her eyes she threw herself at her father, just like when she was a child. He caught her in a warm embrace, also thinking of her childhood leaps into his arms.

"I love you, Papasama!" was all she could say.

"You make Mama and I so very proud. You have been such a good daughter, always living up to your responsibilities and honoring our family ahead of your own wishes. But now it is time for you to fly away, like a bird kicked out of the nest."

He paused, gently easing Sumiko back onto her own feet before continuing. "Now, I am off to the sento for my bath. I'll be home in about two hours. Unless you have other plans, I want you to join Mama and I for some tea when I get back from the Sento. Mama is making some strawberry daifuku and we have some Belgian chocolates from the Yamadas. While we have our koucha, you can tell us about your plans and what we can do to help you make this dream into a reality."

Sumiko could not say a word. All she could do was nod her head excitedly as the tears began to well up and flow over her smiling, happy face.

She watched her father as he headed down the lane towards the sento. Humming his favorite song to himself, he seemed to be perfectly content. It was as if he was reflecting on a perfect moment that had been long awaited for, that had gone according to plan.

2

INTERNATIONAL CENTER

For a few panicked seconds Sumiko thought that she had left David's present at home. It was a modest gift, simply a traditional collage of folded paper and simply sketched lines depicting one of the floats of the Gion Festival. There was also a small photo album of David's visits to the Nishijin

Textile Center on Horikawa Dori, not far from the Kichida family home.

David had made quite an impression on the staff on his first visit as a substitute teacher. He had gone on to teach a conversational English class at the Textile Center ever since.

That's where she had first met David, her very own English Teacher from Canada. Miyuki Yamaguchi, Sumiko's best friend, had invited Sumiko to join the Nishijin group as they went on an excursion with David, helping to hang decorative fabrics on some of the Hook and Yuma floats in last year's Gion Festival. After that Sumiko had joined one of David's more advanced conversational English classes at the International Center.

David was from Yellowknife, in the Northwest Territories. He had shared his pictures and stories about life in the Northwest Territories with the class, making for some interesting discussions. Ever since then Sumiko had been in love.

She was not in love with David, far from it. He was not her type at all. Sumiko was in love with Canada. It fit with her childhood love for nature and her yearning to fly away, over the rainbow. The clincher may have been a photograph David had shown the class, of a commercial aircraft at the airport in Yellowknife. Painted on its tail was something that looked like a rainbow, only more energetic – the dancing colors of the northern lights, the *aurora borealis*.

Ever since then, visiting Yellowknife and other places she had learned about in Canada had been her dream. The more she researched all the things to see and do in that massive country, the more detailed her fantasy had become. The more her friends and social contacts had told her about their own adventures on summer trips to Canada and the United States, the more real her fantasy became with every passing day. Someday soon, she too would travel to Canada! .

As her father had said, this fantasy had started years ago when she had become fascinated with the forests and natural beauty she had seen in movies like *Always, True Grit* and *Pale Rider*. This early love of forests, grasslands and mountains had also contributed to her chosen field of studies, environmental quality management engineering.

With her father and mother now solidly behind her and supportive of her plan to go on a year-long homestay trip to Vancouver, Sumiko felt as though a heavy load had been lifted off of her shoulders.

Her last month at home getting ready for her trip had been a busy time. She carefully packed as much as she could into the sturdy backpack she had bought specially for this trip.

Now, with just a few days to go before her trip and with each last-minute task completed before her departure date of 01 November, Sumiko's anticipation grew ever stronger.

Finding the photo album and gift safe and sound in her handbag, Sumiko felt a wave of relief wash over her. She enjoyed the remainder of the ride on the Tozai Line of the Kyoto Municipal Subway System as though for the last time.

As she listened to someone trying to talk in English, making all the pronunciation and grammatical errors that Japanese typically made, Sumiko realized that the streetcar had already reached the Kyoto International Center of Languages, in the Sakyo-ku area on the east side of the city. Stepping off the subway along with a small group of students and their native English speaking friend, Sumiko hung back and followed the group, listening in discretely.

As she listened in on their conversation, she wondered what level they had attained on the English Placement Tests. She suspected that they might have reached at least one level higher than she had. Her own interest in actually learning English had only began in the last year. Before that, Sumiko had not put any real effort into her English studies, even if she had long planned to do so. She had been far too busy with school. The plan had always been to devote her full attention to her English studies once her university studies were completed.

Now, with her trip to Canada just a few weeks away, she felt ashamed at having put so little effort into her high school English classes and no effort at all throughout her university days. She felt woefully unprepared.

She knew, from her conversational English classes over the past year that she would have difficulties at the start of her trip abroad. Like so many young Japanese girls, Sumiko had excellent book knowledge of English. She had a solid grasp of English vocabulary and grammatical rules but to her teacher's great frustration she had a real problem that had not been solved. She was simply too hesitant to actually speak, to compose and utter sentences out loud, to communicate naturally. Putting her thoughts into voice was a barrier that Sumiko wanted to overcome, but had so far the solution to this problem had been elusive.

David had tried everything from audio taped dialogues and web-based dialogue simulations to pen-pal clubs and even to introducing Sumiko to unattached English speaking 'ExPat' friends of his. None of this had worked, however, as Sumiko would simply shut down and become extremely shy, unable to communicate in a natural way.

Sumiko believed that she could do it, somehow, if she was truly forced to. Her goal was to be so isolated from other Japanese people during her homestay that she would be forced to find the way to communicate effectively in English. She was certain that her solid grasp of vocabulary and grammar would allow her language skills to flourish, and she was grateful to David and the other teachers at the International Center for all of their perseverance with her.

At the end of her final class, when it was time for the class to give their weekly eBook oral reports, Sumiko knew it was her last chance to test her speaking skills. When the time came for her to stand up and give her own report, she was ready. With the same flushed face and nervous voice as always, Sumiko began.

"Weekly eBook journal, by Sumiko Kichida. This week, in my eBook about Emelia Earhart, I read a chapter about her first solo flight."

"A woman should not flying airplanes, that man work!" interrupted Tadao, the class clown.

"Tadao-kun, you are such a jerk," said Miyuki, Sumiko's loyal friend, one of the more popular girls in the class. "Sumiko listened to your report on monstrous trucks, so why don't you shutdown and hear to her reportings!"

"Aah, the expression is 'Shut Up', Miyuki, and it's not polite to say that to a classmate," said David.

"OK, sumimasen, I am sorry, that was rudely of me, please continuing story," said Tadao.

"Arigato, gozaimasu, Tadao-kun," Sumiko said, sarcastically to the annoying boy. Sumiko finished her report with a stronger voice than David had heard in a long time. Rather than correct her many grammatical errors, David decided to just let her keep going. Sumiko was on a roll and had some real momentum going. He figured that her ego needed a bit of a positive boost. But when she told the class that this would be her last time

27

with them, as she was off to 'Bankoobah', David had to say something.

"That was great, Sumiko! You can e-mail me your report and I'll send back my corrections. But I have to say, you really need to fix how you pronounce your 'V's. Can you say the name of the city you are going to, only this time more carefully?"

"Ban-Ku-Burr. No! Choto-matte! Van-Koo-Burr?" She became embarrassed and clammed up, then suddenly felt a wave of insight and excitement. "No! V! V! V! V! Now I can feel it! Like you say many time, V make lips va-va-va-vibrate, but 'B' not bibrate. V is Very Vibrating! Vancouver has a V! So it's Van-Koo-Ver!" she said, excitedly.

"That's right, you've finally got it, Sumiko!"

"Thanks. It's berry important that I say it right!"

"V. V. V. Very important, Sumichan," said one of the girls, encouragingly.

"Yes, it is very important to say Vancouver correctly! Thank you very much, Kyoko-San."

"So tell us all about your homestay plan, and don't worry about any mistakes. Just let the words flow out of your heart," said David.

"OK. Well, first of all I take Haruka train from Kyoto Station to Kansai International Airport - KIX.

I am flying Japan Air Lines, so I can check my bags in here at train station in Kyoto at JAL counter and not have to handle again bags until I am arrived Ban-," Sumiko caught herself and then continued, "Vancouver. Then my homestay family will meet me to arrivals terminal and I finally met them." Sumiko warmed to her topic and pulled out her wallet as she continued, "Do you want to see their picture? This homestay Papasan. He name Doctor Sean Goodwin. He like me, engineer, but he has PHD because he very older than my have. So we can will having lot of dialoguings about solar powering panels, ceramic engines and other thing I knowing somethings about. This Mamasan, Jennifer Goodwin. She working bakery and ESL teacher adding to being Mama. This my homestay sister, Katie. She has just 12 years age. That good because my little sister also 12 has, so will really be just exactly same like my real family. And this tall boy homestay brother, Andrew. His are 17 olds. I don't know what like having brother, so I am really exciting! But from their website I seed that he expert snowboardering and skiinger on Whistler Mountain. That where they had Vancouver Olympics two thousand and ten years. So maybe I can will go some of the Olympicsing places like going skating and places that our Japanese athletes like Mao Asada and Keiichiro Nagashima got their skating medals!" Sumiko paused, not sure what to say next.

Grimacing from all of the articles that Sumiko had left out and the many other errors she made, David had to continue to let them slide. He wanted to encourage her to keep pouring her heart out unselfconsciously. "How long will you be there?"

"One year for, David San, and then I am probably returned to Kyoto."

"Probably?" asked David.

Embarrassed at giving away a little secret, Sumiko tried to change the subject. "My ticket for one year and I have studenting visa, but maybe I finding work or study longer than one year. I not know how future holding at me, but I hopeful to successful experiencing."

After the excited speech, the longest, most natural and spontaneous speech she had ever made, the sudden frown on her face was a surprise to everybody in the class.

"What's wrong, Sumiko? Why do you suddenly look unhappy?" asked David.

"I don't want say. It very personality".

"You mean personal?"

"It's because she does not plan come home at all!" said Tadao. "Sumiko plannings find some Canadian guy and never come back to Japan! I heard her telling Miyuki!"

In tears, Sumiko ran out of the classroom. Miyuki gave Tadao a harsh look. The rest of the class sat in silent shock.

Two hours later, when he was packing his teaching materials up after the last class for the evening, David was surprised to see Sumiko return to the classroom.

"Sumiko! I'm so glad you came back. I have something for you," David handed her a letter.

"What are it?" she said, nervously accepting the thick envelope with both hands as though it were highly valuable, like the cash bonus and thank you card that her father handed out to each and every member of his research team during the company meetings she had attended over the years. But it is extremely rare for an English teacher to give a gift to a student, and generally not appropriate.

"It's a collection of short exercises to review on your long flight across the Pacific Ocean. They're simple dialogues you have done before, but geared to your travel itinerary. I also included some information about Yellowknife, because you seemed to be very interested in my hometown. Just make sure to take a dogsled ride, see the northern lights, go ice-fishing and try some of the other activities I wrote about for you in your package. There's also a letter of introduction for you, if you decide to join the Japanese – Canadian language exchange club at the Vancouver Mokuyokai Society. I think it would be good for you to get involved there as a volunteer Japanese teacher to someone who can work with you on your English in exchange. It's a great way to meet some native English speakers, and I don't mean just the boys!"

Very embarrassed at that last comment, Sumiko put a hand up to cover her red face. "Thank you, David San, I looking in front to look through this materials."

"Looking forward to…," David said.

"Thanks. 'Looking forward.' Can I continuing send you my eBook reportings? Will you write me?" she asked, meekly.

"Sure, I'd love to. And if you upload some pictures of your adventure I will post them on the International Center's website. In fact, if you agree, we could make a blogsite, such as 'homestay-adventure-vancouver.blogspot.com', and you could blog about your adventure as you go. I could use it for our weekly class discussions and get the other students to post replies to your posts."

"That sounds like funny. OK, lets doing that!"

"Yes, that sounds like fun. Let's do that," he repeated, once again subtly correcting her errors.

"And I have gift for you, too. I forget giving you earlier," Sumiko said.

"Great, can I open it now?"

"Sure, please. It's a nothing. But everybody on Nishijin Textile Center still talking about how much they liking your English class. So I put together small photo album about you helping us with Gion festival, and the others gived this framed hook picture gift your."

Opening the present, the smile on David's face was so genuine and uplifting that Sumiko imagined how wonderful it would be to one day find her own Canada-jin who would smile that way at her.

"This is great! You put everybody's names on it, too. I just love this. Thank you very much, and please pass on my thanks to everybody at Nishijin. Unfortunately I won't be able to return to the factory for quite some time, I have to teach a course in Ishiyama, so I won't be in Kyoto that much for a few months. But I'll try to pop in there eventually, to thank them in person."

"That's good."

"Oh, Sumiko, I was meaning to ask you. How did you choose your homestay family, after all? Have you checked them out, to make sure they are legitimate?"

"What doest 'letigi-mate' mean?"

"Lah-Git-Ee-Mit. It means honest, real."

"Oh. Yes, I finded them in HomestayFinder.com and then I checked them with e-home-stay teacher on Barnaby."

"You mean in Burnaby?"

"Yes. My e-homestay has working this homestay family before, with Japanese and with Kankokujin students. His saying that this family may asked me to sit on baby sometimes, but always pay for that. They live near in Grosse Mountain, where there are Skyline and hike trailings."

"You mean Grouse Mountain. Grouse is a kind of bird. You should look it up on the web. There are lots of things to do up there. But make sure you have good hiking shoes if you try to hike up the Grouse Grind. It is a hiking trail that goes up one kilometer of elevation in just a short, one hour hike. Many tourists try to do it in lousy footwear."

"What does loosy mean?"

"Lau-See. Lousy means not suitable. Like the shoes you are wearing now. If you wear those shoes when you hike up the rocks and dirt of the Grouse Grind, which is this steep," he shows with his hands, about 45 degrees, "then after the hike you will have very sore feet and probably a sprained ankle or two. What you need is a well-fit pair of hiking boots."

"OK, I bringing hiking bootses. Thanks for the advices."

"So just keep in touch with us and have a great time. I'm sure you'll have the time of your life. Oh! I almost forgot, I have something magic to give you for your trip, Sumiko."

"Magic?"

David took something out of his pocket and walked around behind Sumiko. Then his large arms reached around in front of her, and lowered a strange pendant onto her neck, brushing her long hair aside as he did up the clasp.

"What is it?" Sumiko asked, as she pulled it up a bit so that she could see it better. It was a tiny gold pepper shaker, like you would see in a diner.

"It is your magic Article Talisman," he said with a smile.

"Articles?"

"Yes, the little words you forget, which we use extensively in English. You know, the little worlds like 'the', 'a;, 'an', and 'some'. When you are talking in English, just imagine you are shaking your little pepper shaker and these little words will fall out into your sentences like little grains of pepper. Practice by re-reading your last report on Emelia Earhart. I wrote in all the missing articles in red. Just read it over, and shake your Articles-Shaker-Talisman with each article, and you'll see how much pepper you have been missing when you serve up your English sentences."

Sumiko grasped the golden shaker as if it were precious. The articles had long been her Achilles heel, and she was sure that the talisman would help.

"Thank you, David, I will add a the lots of pepperings to the my English."

Smiling at her over-correction, "Great, but remember not to add too much pepper either!"

With that, David seemed to be concerned about the time so Sumiko said her good-bye and hurried out to catch the subway

For the first time ever she felt as though she had just had a complete conversation in English. This time it was not a bunch of rehearsed or memorized phrases from her notebooks, but real words flowing from her heart. She knew that part of this was because she felt so relaxed with David, but another part was that she felt more confident lately. Something in her seemed to be changing.

She did not feel like those silly girls who giggle and laugh at the unusual and at times inappropriate things that Gaijin like David and other teachers do.

She no longer felt any interest in hanging around with her classmates, talking in Japanese all the time. What Sumiko yearned for was more of that intense, deeply personal conversation like she just experienced with David. Talking about things that mattered, things that would improve her life.

Sumiko felt ready for her adventure to begin.

38

3

MY HUMAN DESTINY

It would be her last note to her little sister, and Sumiko knew that her little sister, Aiko, would treasure it. So she took a great deal of care to use simple words in English and to encourage her little sister. It was while she composed the letter, thinking about her little sister, that she had a true epiphany. Her entire family, her Mama, her Papa, and even her little sister had known that one day Sumiko would leave for some English speaking country. Yet none of them had let on to her that they knew it. Little Aikochan had been working so hard at her English classes in elementary school, and was always writing little notes in English in a playful game with her older sister. Now it all made sense. Aiko wanted to be a part of whatever Sumiko was going to do with her life.

Now, on the eve of her departure, Sumiko finally understood just how deeply her departure would affect the Kichida family and especially her baby sister.

A tear came to her eye that night as she composed that last note. It took Sumiko over an hour to write it. She had to check her English dictionary and grammar guide several times. The letter had to be perfect. When she thought that she was finished, she remembered the talisman David had given her and sprinkled a few more articles into every sentence. When she was done, the note read more like English than her past attempts; the pepper had worked its magic.

"Aikochan, I have left for my homestay in Vancouver. I will miss you so much. You are my best friend, little sister. And now you are the one who must take care of Mama and Papa. I know you can do it, you are wise well beyond your years, and you are truly good. I will think about you every morning and every night. When I need your help, I will look at the pictures you gave me to carry in my purse. And I will look at the Big Dipper, the Hokuto Shichisei Enmei-Kyo. I will follow my Rencho-sho Dragon star on the handle, go into the cup for your Rokuzon-sho Tiger star and then follow Domon-sho to Donro-sho and beyond until I find Hokkyokusei, the North Star. While I look at Polaris late at night in Canada it will be early morning for you, just when the alarm goes off to wake you up for school. So if you rush out of bed and look to the north and find Hokkyokusei, you and I will be connected at that moment. And just like the Big Dipper controls one's destiny, even if you and I are separated by a great distance, our destinies are linked. You and I will always be like connected, forever.

I will write letters to you, just like this one, and mail them whenever I can. Start looking for them in the mail starting next week. Gambatte kudasai. Love Sumiko."

Sumiko slipped the letter into the center of Aiko's futon, still rolled up after the family got up and Sumiko had walked Aiko to school. It was their customary way to send notes to each other, little surprises to discover before bedtime.

They had shared a tearful goodbye. Sumiko was nearly heartbroken when she saw Aiko holding back her own tears, and when she had said "Ne-chan, older sister, promise you will not forget me!"

And then Aiko had turned abruptly and disappeared into her school, not looking back.

Sumiko was so proud of her baby sister, who had been strong for both of them.

Sumiko later visited the miniature Shinto shrine in her neighborhood. She put a few coins in the collection box, hung a wooden Ema tablet upon which she had hand-painted a wish for the safety and success of her family, rang the small bell hanging from the shrine and then solemnly clapped her hands twice to attract the attention of the Kami spirits of the shrine. She then contemplated her prayer for a few minutes and meditated on each and every one of her loved ones.

Sumiko was sincere in her practice of the uniquely Japanese combination of Shinto and Buddhism, even if she was not a deeply religious person. To her, a profound respect for the spirits of her ancestors was not in any way in conflict with her rational and thoroughly modern world view.

She had no interest in the Christian or Muslim religions, sticking with the traditional Shinto and Buddhist roots of her country. As she thought about the country of her birth she felt great pride in being Japanese. Her country had such a long and proud history and had accomplished so much in the modern era as well.

Sumiko had an internationalist point of view and was more politically aware than her peers. She was proud of her country for standing up to lead the international cooperation on climate change and for advocating for the peaceful settlement of disputes between nations.

But these reflections also made her feel a twinge of guilt for her equally strong views that her future lay elsewhere. This duality, between being proudly Japanese and yet also a citizen of a larger world, at least in her heart, was partly explained by the character of her birth sign. Born on May 22nd, 1989, Sumiko was a Gemini, born in the Japanese year of the Hebi, the Snake. This explained the dual nature of her personality. She could be serious and reserved at some times and then a playful risk-taker at other times. She had all the characteristics of someone born in the year of the Snake: Sumiko was a deep thinker, very wise, lucky with money and also extremely determined.

As she walked home that evening, Sumiko felt like she was ready to take on the world, that she could do anything. In this state of mind, after paying her respects to her ancestors and making the appropriate gestures at the shrine, Sumiko was ready to step out onto the world stage.

4

A CHANGE OF CLIMATE

Sumiko's father had accompanied her to the train station in Kyoto. On the subway platform, Sumiko had an interesting experience. Standing for a moment on the last step on the way down to the subway platform on the Karasuma Line, she had looked out across the sea of heads.

The platform was nearly full of well-dressed businessmen, all making their way to their office jobs. It was a veritable sea of identical salarymen, all no more than five foot six tall, all with the same black hair. She looked at individual men to see who might be a chikan, a subway pervert who would take advantage of the crowded conditions of the subway cars to press up against unsuspecting women. It had happened to her more than once, and made her do everything she could to avoid travelling on the subways during peak hours.

She looked at the tired faces of some of the ladies, wondering if any of them had regrets over their choice of a career rather than a family. Then she looked at a very tall man at the extreme end of the platform. His skin was as black as shoe leather. With a bit of embarrassment, Sumiko wondered if what they said about black men was true. Then she saw him looking her way. She looked away in embarrassment, turning her head to her left. There in front of her, no more than a meter away, was a tall white man. She could see that he was sweating, as if he had been running to make to the train in time.

He looked uncomfortable in his business suite, as though he was not accustomed to wearing a tie. Then she noticed that he too was looking out across the sea of Japanese people, all much shorter than himself. Her mind automatically calculated and determined that the white man was looking at the black man. At just that moment, the white man smiled. Sumiko could not help herself, she had to know. She looked back towards the large African man. He, too, was smiling.

It was as if the two men had both looked across the sea of identical Japanese business men, feeling isolated and out of place being non-Japanese, and their eyes had met. In their look into each other's eyes the two men had exchanged a knowing look that said: *Brother, I have more in common with you than I do with any of this crowd of Japanese commuters!*

Sumiko suddenly felt some kind of connection with the two men. Somehow she felt as if she was no longer part of the 'A-Set-O' or 'B-Set-O' lives that Japanese people are constrained to fit into. She was now a stranger in a strange land, on her way home to a land she had never visited.

Riding in the Haruka train from Kyoto to KIX, Kansai International Airport, Sumiko felt as though she was flying, just like her heroine, Amelia Earhart. Her train curved gracefully around the larger obstacles as it zoomed along just over the rooftops of the smaller buildings. The high-speed train did not have that clickety-clack of the old-style trains. The quiet, smooth ride made Sumiko think about the airplane journey to come.

She had flown on mid-sized jets on her vacations to places like Seoul and Hong Kong, but she had never been in a wide-body jet. She looked forward with anticipation to riding in the beautiful bird-like Japan Air Lines Boeing 747-400.

As the train curved around the final turn and began to plunge downward into the KIX Station Sumiko had a good look at the row of as many as 24 massive aircraft all laid out in a row at their gates. She looked towards the aircraft imagining all of the exotic places that these aircraft were bound for.

After checking in and having the clerk confirm that the suitcases had already been transferred from the train through to the aircraft, Sumiko appreciated the clean and efficient operations at KIX. Most Japanese take such things for granted, living in the most technologically sophisticated nation on earth.

The only negative sentiment she experienced on the trip from Kyoto to KIX was the way the sky looked as the train passed through the more built up area of Osaka. In the lower reaches of the Kansai plain, the air was brown. Pollution from China and other Southeast Asian nations, as well as that of Osaka itself, had concentrated in the still air of an unseasonably hot fall day. She saw numerous people wearing gauze masks, standing on the train platforms as the express Haruka sped past without stopping.

For a few minutes Sumiko's heart sank with thoughts of how badly humanity is treating the environment and how disappointed she was that world leaders had failed to follow-through on the Kyoto Protocol of 1997. She had a momentary flash of memory of a time when she was about nine years old. She had asked her father what was so important on the news. He had explained to her that the world had come to Kyoto to save the planet. Even at such an early age, Sumiko understood how important it was to protect nature and how bad it was to pollute. Taking the lead from her father, ever since then she been proud of her nation's role. Japan had tried to turn the tide, to encourage the nations of the world to set some meaningful goals that would curb the growth in carbon dioxide pollution, and potentially save humankind from itself.

As she looked across the ugly brown sky looming over the Kansai Plain she knew that the world had largely abandoned the Kyoto Protocol.

Even the country of her dreams, with all of its beautiful natural spaces, had disappointed the world. She was ashamed for Canada, one of the worst per-capita polluting nations, for more than doubling carbon emissions in the years since signing the Kyoto protocol.

It seemed ironic to Sumiko that she was leaving a heavily polluted country that was committed to reducing its carbon footprint and heading for a seemingly pristine climate in a country that had largely abandoned its responsibilities to protect the environment.

How strange, Sumiko thought to herself, how different this would be. What would it be like for her in Canada? What could she learn, and could she somehow make a difference there? The sinking in her heart was replaced with the resolve and the courage of a young traveller embarking on her great voyage into the world.

5

A HELPING HAND, MATE

It sounded like English, but something was wrong with the way the man talked. Sumiko had nothing to do for the two hours before her flight would board so she had been wandering around the massive international departure terminal, with all sorts of thoughts in her mind. When she had encountered the middle-aged western couple she could not help herself from trying to identify their unusual accent. It sounded like English, but only barely so. They seemed to be having trouble.

Feeling adventurous and anonymous, Sumiko thought that maybe she could help them. "Herro, do you need me helping?"

"G'day, missie, how ya goin? Yes. We can't figure this out. Our ticket says 'Gate D-42', but we've been back and forth along this bugger of a terminal at least half a dozen times - nothing like

'D-42' anywhere, and we've only got a few minutes before our departure time. I tell you what, I'm getting right cheesed off!"

The man seemed distraught; his wife utterly exhausted. After taking a couple of seconds to look at their First Class ticket, Sumiko quickly understood the problem. The couple simply had not crossed to the correct side of the terminal. Perhaps the signage could have been better, or maybe the large terminal had intimidated the poor old couple, but she felt confident that she understood where they needed to be. Just to make sure, she took a look at the television monitors that showed aircraft departures and gates. Sure enough, there was a Qantas Airlines flight boarding for Sidney at Gate D-42 on the other side of the terminal. All they had to do was cross from the predominantly Japan Air Lines side to the other side, where there were foreign carriers.

"Come that way with me. Your departure gate is not far away."

"Cheers, missie. That's right cordial of you!"

"Do you see this Kanji on your ticket?"

"What's a Kan Gee?" asked the man.

"Kanji is the Japanese word for Chinese character. They are simply pictures that have meaning. Like this one on your ticket. You see? What does it look like to you?" Sumiko asked, smiling mischievously as she led them towards D-42.

"It looks like a par of doors into a saloon!" the man said.

"What is saloon?" asked Sumiko as she and the couple reached the gate where the cabin crew of the Qantas flight were processing the last of their passengers.

"A saloon is where an ocker can get a drink. You know, like in John Wayne movies. A bar," he explained.

"Oh, yes. Well, that's exactly what this Kanji says. It is a doorway, like into your salon. Or in this case, your departure gate."

"You mean saloon. Yes, I can see that now. Well, I wish someone had told me that it was this easy. After two days visiting Japan, you are the first real person we have had a conversation with. Other than hotel staff, everybody here seems to clam up when we talk to them. It's as if they don't understand the Queen's English!"

"Well, your English is a bit unusual. Are you from Australia?" asked Sumiko.

"South Australia, actually, Adelaide. The Barossa Valley to be precise. Home of some of the finest wines what will ever wet your whistle," the man said with great pride. "Clarke's the name, Jocko Clarke!" His big hand nearly crushed her small hand as he shook her hand in his. "And this Sheila is my better half, Andrea."

"Very nice to meet you. My name Sumiko."

"Pleased to meet you too, Sue."

Sumiko noticed that his yellow and green golf shirt had custom embroidery over his heart. It was a strange combination of a golden cross surmounted by a four-pointed silver star. In the center was what looked like a purple flower, perhaps a thistle. Surrounding this was a phrase that did not make any sense to Sumiko, but looked like: '*NEMO ME IMPUNE LACESSIT.*'

Sumiko thought that it could be in Latin, but it really made an impression on her. Such a lovely design embroidered onto his shirt, it must be very important to him. Perhaps it has something to do with his family or a club he is a member of, she thought to herself.

"What meaning?" Sumiko stammered, trying to find the words to form her question.

Jocko followed her eyes to his chest and immediately understood. With a twinkle in his eye he said in a very strange accent, "Whah doors meddle whi me!" and then he smiled as he winked an eye at her confused face.

He had just opened his mouth to explain when their conversation was suddenly interrupted by the airport's public address system.

"Final boarding call for Qantas Airlines Flight 407 to Sydney, Australia. All passengers should now have boarded at Gate D-42. Paging Mr. and Mrs. Clarke, please proceed to Gate D-42. Your aircraft is about to depart."

The message was repeated in Japanese, which seemed ridiculous to Sumiko.

"That's us, darling. We have to run. It was a real pleasure to talk with you, Sue" Jocko Clarke said, "And here's my business card. Look us up if you are ever down under, come and see us. Just give us a shout on the blower and we'll set out some right dinkum tuck for you, lassie! Cheeirio!" he said, as he and his wife hurried off to their gate.

Sumiko did not understand much of his final words to her but she smiled as she listened to

Jocko and Mrs Clarke squabbling as they rushed off.

"You're such a gas bag, Jocko, a real yobbo!"

"Oh stop your grizzle, darling! Make tracks!"

Sumiko waived at the nice couple as they rushed to their gate, much to the relief of the Qantas Airlines flight attendant who was holding the door open for them.

With a smile on her face, Sumiko turned towards her own gate. It was a real confidence builder for her, having helped a couple using her very own English skills.

Sumiko also felt badly that the Clarkes had not spoken much with regular Japanese people. It was not their fault, she knew. Japanese people tended to clam up and shy away from strangers. It was a deeply ingrained trait in Japanese culture, avoiding the strange or the foreign. But for that old couple it probably meant that they had not made any meaningful connections with Japan or with any Japanese people. What a shame, thought Sumiko. And with that, she vowed to herself to break through such barriers at every opportunity.

6

BOTTLE OF WINE

It was a coincidence that was not lost on Sumiko, and she took it as yet another positive omen for her trip. It had all started before the aircraft even started engines. She had been seated in an aisle seat near the middle of the aircraft when one of the cabin crew approached. Speaking in Tokyo accented Japanese, Mrs. Ohayashi, Senior Purser according to her nametag, told Sumiko that the aircraft was inadvertently overbooked and that she needed to reassign Sumiko to another seat. Mrs. Ohayashi had a mischievous twinkle in her eye as she waited for Sumiko to comply.

Sumiko instantly liked and trusted this lady. Without hesitation, Sumiko replied in very polite Japanese. "Yes, right away, where am I going?"

"Just follow me, Ojousan!"

As she followed the Flight Attendant, Sumiko imagined how adventurous life must be for a member of an international flight crew. It must be nice to stay in fancy hotels all around the world, meeting interesting international travelers and taking trips anywhere in the world as a side benefit of their job. What a life that must be, she thought to herself.

Suddenly Sumiko grew concerned. There must be some mistake. Mrs. Ohayashi was leading her into the First Class cabin! Several of the seats were empty, unlike the very crowded main section of the aircraft.

"Sit here, you have been upgraded to First Class, Ojousan. You are now a movie star. Enjoy!"

Sumiko was dumbstruck. She could barely mutter "Arigato gozaimasu!" as she took the indicated seat. It was a window seat. As she looked outside onto the airport pavement, where small trains of baggage carts rushed about with suitcases of every color and design imaginable, Sumiko realized that because she was sitting so far towards the front of the aircraft she would have a superb view of Osaka Bay as the aircraft departed. She would also have great sight-lines to view Georgia Strait as the aircraft arrived in Vancouver. What fabulous luck!

As Sumiko settled in to her very pleasant First Class seat she began to size up the other people in First Class. Most were wealthy Japanese. A few were well-dressed foreigners. One of the westerners looked a bit familiar, but she could not remember where she might have seen her before.

Then Mrs. Ohayashi led a young man to a seat a few rows ahead. Thanking Mrs. Ohayashi in English, the man said: "This is perfect! I'm on my way home to my bride. We were just married two weeks ago and I had to rush off to Osaka for a shoot. Our honeymoon was interrupted but as soon as we land we're going to pick up where we left off, and I'm riding First Class all the way to her!"

"Are you a photographer?" asked Mrs. Ohayashi.

"Yes, I work for Insight Magazine," he said, as he took his seat. Sumiko turned her attention to figuring out how operate the seat's controls. She giggled when she accidentally set of the fully reclined mode, unable to stop the seat as it rotated all the way back to the horizontal and became a comfortable little bed. What luxury! Eventually Mrs. Ohayashi came by and showed Sumiko how to return her chair to an upright position.

During the long flight, while Sumiko worked through some of the dialogues that David had assembled for her, she realized that she had made more than a few mistakes in her conversation with the Australian couple. But that did not take any of the fun away from it. It had made it that much more delightful, in fact. Now she finally understood what David had often tried to explain to the class. He always said: "Whenever you make a mistake in English, you are on the right track! The more mistakes you make, the more progress you are making. So go on out there and collect as many mistakes as you can. Be reckless!"

It is in this process of throwing it out there, composing sentences from the heart or in response to the situation - not by thinking of them in your mind in Japanese and then translating - that you liberate your English. This thought made Sumiko look forward to arriving in Canada. She could really begin to collect mistakes and thereby become fluent in English in no time at all.

As she was sitting there thinking about the Australians, her intuition spoke to her. She felt that something was happening. She looked around, trying to try to figure it out. She saw the flight attendant bring a bottle of wine to the photo-journalist. He accepted the bottle and gave her back two empties, laughing out loud as if he was enjoying a private joke, or just giddy at travelling in First Class and having as much free wine as he could drink.

When Sumiko squinted her eyes in an attempt to get a clear look at the bottle, Mrs. Ohayashi noticed. Moments later, she offered Sumiko an identical bottle.

Sumiko could feel her intuition almost screaming at her but she still had not figured it out. Something about the bottle of wine was important. She read the label: "Thistle & Clarke Shiraz/Cabernet – 2010. Gold Medal Winner, 36th Barossa Wine Show, Adelaide South Australia, March, 11, 2012".

And then she realized what her subconscious was trying to tell her. This wine was from the Barossa Valley and she had helped the owner of the vineyard, Jocko Clarke, find his flight home to Australia!

She smiled to herself as she took out Jocko's business car, his meishi, and compared the embossed logo on the business card with that of the wine bottle. They were identical.

This was the first time in her life that she had interacted that closely with anybody even a little bit famous. Yet another positive omen.

Coincidence is one thing, but what happened next brought the entire event to an even higher level of synchronicity—meaningful coincidence. Just at that moment a magazine fell out of the lap of a sleeping passenger across the aisle from Sumiko. As the copy of Insight Magazine crashed to the floor it opened to a random page. Sumiko picked up the magazine, intending to pass it back to the sleeping traveler. But then she glanced at it. There was a picture of Jocko and Andrea, smiling happily!

Sumiko took a closer look at the photograph and saw that there was a huge pile of wine crates stacked up all around Jocko and his wife. Jocko was shaking hands with a well-dressed Japanese business man. In Jocko's other hand was a bottle of wine.

The caption read: "Mr. Masaru Kobayashi, CEO of Japan Air Lines, accepts the first bottle of the highly prized Australian wine from Mr. John Clarke, owner of Thistle & Clarke vineyards. As part of a strategy to attract more sophisticated air travelers, Japan Air Lines has completely reorganized their First Class menus, upgrading the airline to the equivalent of a Five Star hotel. The new menu and wine list will officially begin on the Osaka to Vancouver route, starting this Friday."

Sumiko was utterly astounded. All of her superstitions, her intuition and her sense of destiny told her that this was so much more than a coincidence. The unseen forces that had made her cross paths with Mr. Clarke, on the opening flight of his best wines, and her being upgraded so that she could share in the momentous occasion, was such an unlikely event, such a stroke of good luck, that Sumiko was convinced that it was it was an excellent omen for her journey.

Almost eighteen hours after leaving Osaka, the aircraft was in descent for Vancouver. For most of the passengers it had been a long and grueling flight but for Sumiko, it had been very pleasant. She had enjoyed a five star seven course meal in First Class. On her plate, the meal had been perfectly matched with the fine bottle of award-winning red wine from Australia, from the vineyard of her new Australian friend, Jocko Clarke.

Very pleased at what the universe had provided for her, she had slept for a good six hours in the reclining bed-seat after having completed most of the dialogues that David had given her in Kyoto.

The jumbo jet continued to descend through the clouds and then suddenly it was as if the clouds disappeared and she could see the ground.

There was a long peninsula jutting out into the ocean. It took her a few minutes before she could figure out where she was. And then it hit her, that five-finger map of Vancouver that she had read about in one of the articles in David's package about Vancouver. The article said that the Vancouver area is easy to understand if you simply look at your right hand.

The little finger is the North Shore, the cities of West Vancouver and North Vancouver, and this is where the mountains are. The mountains are lit up at night because ski resorts with powerful lights for night skiing are up there,. From anywhere you are, if you look up at the lights on the North Shore mountains, then you will be looking north, towards that baby finger on your right hand.

One of those mountains, the middle one, is Grouse Mountain, where there are restaurants and shops. In the summer you can hike up the Grouse Grind trail and then spend the day exploring the ski resort and enjoy a wonderful view of the city of Vancouver.

Between that baby finger and the right handed ring finger, where Russians and other Orthodox people wear wedding rings, she knew, there was Burrard Inlet. That is the deep waterway that the cruise ships and commercial ships sail through to enter the port of Vancouver. Sumiko remembered that you can take a small passenger ferry, the SeaBus, right across Burrard Inlet and get a tour of the waterway and all the ships, with nice views of the mountains and the city skyline.

On the North Shore you can shop for fruit and souvenirs at the Lonsdale Quay Market on that baby finger.

Then you take the 'SeaBus' back and you are on the right ring finger again. That is where Stanley Park and downtown Vancouver are. Stanley Park is a big forest park right in the heart of the city. It is surrounded by the 8-km long 'SeaWall' jogging and bicycle path. There is an aquarium, a steam engine ride and a beautiful flower garden in the park. On nice days, artists are in the park selling their paintings and other artwork.

As Sumiko continued comparing the fingers of her right hand with what she could see out the window, she saw the buildings of downtown, and clearly make out Stanley Park. The fingers of land and the waterways that separated them, all made sense to her.

That longest piece of land, jutting out into what must be Georgia Strait, that is the middle finger, she realized. So the tip of that middle finger is where the University of British Columbia and Pacific Spirit Regional Park are. Sure enough, when she looked out the window to compare, she could see the forest of the Pacific Spirit Park and the clusters of buildings that made up the University of British Columbia. So that north shoreline of that middle finger, that must be Spanish Banks and Jericho Beach. That would be where all the windsurfing, sailing and sun-bathing she had read about takes place, she thought to herself excitedly! For a moment she imagined herself taking a stroll down one of Vancouver's many beaches on a hot summer day

With a smile she looked at the end of the finger nail, where she knew the nudist beach, 'Wreck Beach', must be. May be one day she would have the courage to go there. May be not completely nude, but possibly topless, she thought to herself and her cheeks started to blush.

Then she identified an arm of the Fraser River, which separated the main residential area of Vancouver from the airport and Richmond. She knew that Richmond was a very Chinese suburb of Vancouver.

The aircraft made a graceful turn to line up with the runway and the airport moved past her window towards the front of the aircraft and out of her view.

She looked down at her right hand, at the index finger. That's the airport and Richmond, she figured. There is an elevated 'SkyTrain' subway connection from the airport, here on the index finger, crossing over the river and through a tunnel under the middle finger, and then on to the right-ring finger of downtown. For such a cosmopolitan city, Vancouver's three or four SkyTrain lines seemed pretty small in comparison to any Japanese city. But then again, most Canadians must drive big SUVs, Sports Utility Vehicles, and do not use mass transit, she reminded herself.

She looked across the First Class cabin, peering past other passengers to see what she could see through the right side windows. Sure enough, she could see the ferry terminal. That's the thumb, the southern-most part of the Vancouver region. That's where you take a ferry boat to visit Victoria, the very English city on Vancouver Island.

Sumiko had read all about the famous flower garden called 'Butchart Gardens', the beautiful and historic Empress Hotel and the British Columbia Museum. She looked forward to one day riding the ferry to Vancouver Island. Maybe, she thought, she would even see a pod of Killer whales as they swam through the Strait of Georgia.

As long as she had her right hand with her, Sumiko would always know where she was in the Vancouver area. Unless of course it was one of those grey, rainy days when you can't see the mountains at all! She smiled at that, because as a child she had always loved to play in puddles .

Moments later the aircraft had landed and was taxiing in to the terminal. She had made it, she had arrived in Vancouver. Now the adventure would really begin!

Little did she know just how dramatic and life-changing her adventure was about to become.

7

ANYTHING TO DECLARE?

Sumiko strode eagerly off of the aircraft and walked up the gantry into the terminal.

Once clear of the other passengers she moved off to one side to get her luggage. She could feel her heart racing, beating loudly in her chest. To calm herself, she took a few deep breaths as she looked around.

From the flow of people, all moving towards her right, she quickly figured out which way she had to go and followed the other passengers towards the Canada Customs and Immigration desk. She saw other passengers rushing towards small tables where they filled out some cards and then hurried towards the Immigration Officers.

Sumiko soon understood why they had been in such a rush. Within minutes there was a throng of passengers lined up, some of whom she recognized from her flight. One in particular, the woman she had seen in First Class, seemed to be very concerned about how she looked. She kept looking at a tiny mirror in her hands.

Sumiko found one of the cards that the other passengers had filled out, and read it. It was a Customs Declaration. There were a series of questions asking if she had brought various items with her into the country. It took her several minutes to fill the form out, until she learned that there was a Japanese sample under the plastic sheet on the table. That simplified things for her, and she realized that she had nothing to declare.

When it was finally her turn to show the Customs and Immigration Officer her Japanese passport and her Canada Student Visa. She handed over the Customs Declaration Card. Sumiko worried that the Immigration Officer might ask her some complicated questions that she would not understand. But all he asked was "Anything to declare?"

"Nothing to declare," answered Sumiko.

"Welcome to Canada," replied the Officer, handing back her documents and turning his attention to the next person in line.

After putting her documents safely into her travel pouch she followed the English and French signage to the arrivals areas where she found a baggage carousel with her JAL flight number displayed on the electronic sign above the carousel. After a short wait her packsack came up out of the tunnel and then tumbled down to the steel ring of the oval shaped carousel.

She pulled her packsack up and set it on the ground in front of her. After stuffing her notebook into a small carry-on bag connected to the straps on her pack, she hefted the sturdy rucksack onto her shoulder. With her pack on her back and her hands now free, Sumiko was ready to go. With a quick look around to see where the other passengers were flowing to next, she set off after them through the automatic glass doors and was suddenly confronted with a throng of photographers snapping pictures of her.

For a moment, it seemed, the paparazzi were interested in Sumiko. After her flight in First Class, it almost made sense. Then she realized that she was standing right beside the red-headed woman from First Class.

The woman had an amused smile on her face, as if she had been looking forward to this moment of attention. She was immediately greeted by a man in a black suit, wearing a hat. He must be a limo driver, assumed Sumiko as she watched the woman follow the man off into the buzzing swarm of paparazzi. She walked with the grace and poise of true royalty, seemingly enjoying being the center of attention.

As the famous woman walked away, Sumiko heard one of the press shout a question: "Who will you be taking to the Oscars, Mrs. Walker?"

And then Sumiko remembered who the important woman was. She was the actress who had been in Tokyo for the screening of her film, "Lost Child", which was expected to fetch her a second Oscar.

And I was sitting right across from her for the last 18 hours, thought Sumiko. She couldn't wait to tell her homestay family about everything that had happened on the flight over the Pacific.

Where were they, anyhow? Sumiko stood there in the greeting area looking at the personalized signs being held up by people all around, such as "Robinson Party", "Camp Elphinstone", "Lee Group", and so many others. There was no sign with her name on it and no sign with her homestay family's name on it either. They must have been delayed, she thought.

Two hours later, sitting by herself on a couch in the arrivals areas, Sumiko had to face reality. They were not coming.

Something must have gone wrong. So she decided to call them at their home in Edgemont Village. She looked for their phone number, and headed to the pay phone.   And then her life changed forever.

8

JOURNEY TO EDMONTON

Sumiko had some Canadian currency, but no coins. She also had a Citibank credit card, which she had already used successfully at the airport. But she could not figure out how to use the pay phone. In Japan, she could simply insert her phone card into the phone and call anywhere she wanted. Or she could use her cell phone. But she had not had her phone reprogrammed to work in Canada yet. She had assumed that she could do that once she had arrived in Canada and settled in.

Sumiko looked at others using the telephones. She saw them depositing change into the phone, dial numbers, and begin talking. It looked pretty straight forward. All she needed was some coins. So now, thought Sumiko, it was time to take care of herself and stop waiting around for her homestay family. She waited until one of the people using the phone hung up and began to move away, and then Sumiko pounced like a cat.

"Excuses me. Can you herrup me? I have money, but I need some...?" Sumiko frowned, momentarily unable to recall the word 'coins'.

"Some what? Coins for the phone?" asked the well-dressed man.

"Hai, yes, that's it. Coins for the terri-phone," she said.

"Sorry, I'm all out of change. Why don't you get some from that magazine shop?" he said.

"OK. Thank you." Sumiko looked at the shop that the man had pointed at, and headed over to it. She decided it would be best to just buy something and see what she got for change. She spent some time looking at magazines and then chose a small package of bubble gum and handed it to the clerk.

"That will be two dollars and ninety cents," said the clerk.

Sumiko thought about it for a minute, trying to do the math in her mind. She caught herself doing the math in Japanese, and then tried to do it in English. Ten cents, that will be all the coins I will get from this. That may not be enough to pay for a telephone call.

"I want more change, and not all in paper, please," she said, nervously.

"What? You need change for the phone or something?"

"Yes, for the terri-phone," she said, as she handed a fifty dollar bill to the clerk.

"Here you go." The clerk handed Sumiko a handful of coins and some paper money.

"Thank you," said Sumiko. But then she froze, sensing something was wrong. She looked at the banknotes in her hand. She saw that two of them were light blue in color, and had a '5' on the corner. So this is what a Canadian Five Dollar Bill looks like, she thought to herself. There was also a purple one, with a '10' in the corner. So that's a Ten Dollar Bill, she thought. Then she looked at the coins in her hand. She could not figure out how much each coin was worth, but it seemed to her that she had been short-changed. She was certain that she had given the clerk one of those red notes, with a '50' on the corner. She had been given a little over twenty dollars in change from her $50 banknote. That is wrong, she thought to herself, *simply wrong*!

This would never happen in Japan, Sumiko thought, but she had heard that it can happen when you travel. If she were more confident in her English skills then she would have confronted the shop keeper. But Sumiko did not want to go back and start an argument which would only end in embarrassment for her. She would have to be more careful in the future, so that this sort of thing does not happen to her again.

Then, from some place deep inside of her, Sumiko felt a wave of anger rising in her. She felt as if her blood would boil if she did not at least try. So she walked right back to the shop and spoke up in as confident and determined voice as she could muster.

"Excuse me. Have you given me the honesty amount?" asked Sumkio.

"Are you accusing me of cheating you? You gave me twenty dollars. You have your change, now go away!" the lady said, in a way that seemed very rude to Sumiko.

"Actually, this addition not many more than twenty dollar," said Sumiko, "and I actually gave you fifty dollar. I see it, there on top of money drawer," Sumiko said, growing more and more angry that the clerk had stolen from her.

The clerk made a blank stare at her. "You go away! I not steal from you," she said, as she took the $50 bill from the cash drawer and put it under a compartment in the cash register. "Go away!"

The sudden anger from the clerk made Sumiko afraid that maybe she had been mistaken. She was almost ready to walk away and give up, when the man she had spoken with at the telephones suddenly appeared beside Sumiko.

"Excuse me, I saw the transaction," he said to the clerk. "This young woman gave you a fifty dollar bill. You gave her about twenty three dollars in change and what, a two dollar candy? And I saw you put away her fifty just now. You have to give her the correct change, right now!" he said.

"Or what?" demanded the clerk.

"Or I will inform the airport administrators that you are defrauding our foreign guests. I do not think that they will take kindly to anything that hurts the reputation of the Vancouver International Airport. In fact, I think I'll also tell the police, and offer to be a witness if this young lady chooses to press charges," he said.

The clerk seemed to think about it, and then quietly handed over a twenty and a five, and then looked away until Sumiko and the man left the store.

"I can't believe she tried to rip you off," he said.

"What means rip off?"

"A 'rip off' is when someone tries to steal from you. You have to watch out for it all the time."

"Yes, I understand. That was a rip off."

"So do you need any help with the telephone?"

"Yes, please. How do you use it?"

"Do you have the number you want to call?"

"Yes, here it is," Sumiko showed him the phone number in her book.

"OK. Here's what you do. First, you pick up the handset and listen for the dial tone. Then put two of these twenty-five cent coins into the phone, and listen for the dial tone to come back. Then dial 1 and then the ten digits of the number. Here, you try."

Sumiko put two of the shiny twenty-five cent coins into the phone, listened to the sound of the dial tone coming back, and then punched in 1-604-555-4138. The phone rang, and then she heard the voice of her homestay mother. She smiled as she recognized the voice.

Seeing that the pretty Japanese girl had gotten through on her call, the man smiled and walked away.

"Hello, you have reached the Goodwin family. We are unable to come to the phone right now, please leave a message."

Sumiko quickly hung up. She did not know what to say, so she did not try to leave a message.

Feeling much more confident now that she understood how to use the pay phone, Sumiko pushed her baggage cart back to the bench she had sat on before, and took out her address book. She read the address of her homestay family. "237 Bonnie Doon Court, Edgemont Village, North Vancouver. V7R 2N4"

Sumiko thought about it for a few minutes, and came up with a plan. She got up, and walked over towards the 'Information' booth.

"Excuse me. How do I get bus to take me at Edgemontont Birrage?" she asked the young girl at the Information kiosk.

"Edgemontont Birrage? Do you mean Edmonton? Edmonton is actually a city, you know, not a village." said the girl.

"Yes, Edgemonton," said Sumiko, thinking that it sounded about right. Maybe it was her pronunciation. She always had troubles with the "L" sound, after all.

"Are you flying to Edmonton?"

"No! I don't want to fly there. I want to take a bus. Where can I find a bus to Edmonton?" asked Sumiko, surprised that there could be an airport near her homestay family. It must be a very small airport, she thought.

"A bus? Well, I guess you could take the SkyTrain to the bus station downtown. Are you sure you are going to Edmonton?"

"Yes, Bonnie Doon neighborhood, Edgemonton," said Sumiko, trying to pronounce the words more carefully.

"Hang on, let me check," the girl said. She typed into her computer, waited a few seconds, and then looked up. "Yes, I Googled it. There is a Bonnie Doon neighborhood in Edmonton. I'm sure they have lots of busses going there from the bus station downtown.

Of course, you could also take the Via Train, it may be a nicer trip for you," She said.

"How do I get to the Via Train?

"Well, you follow those signs to the SkyTrain. You see there?" she pointed.

"Yes, I see, 'SkyTrain'. That is the elevated train to the city?"

"Yes. Take the SkyTrain Canada Line all the way to Granville Station, then change trains for the Expo Line, ride just two stops to the Main Street Station, and as soon as you exit the terminal you will see the Train Station, it's right across the street from the SkyTrain station."

"Thank you, very much".

Sumiko had no trouble following the signs and boarding the SkyTrain. Buying a SkyTrain ticket was as easy as feeding a five dollar bill into the machine, pushing the button for the zone that seemed to be downtown Vancouver, and taking her ticket along with some change from the tray in the ticket vending machine.

With her packsack on her back, she boarded the SkyTrain and sat down in the front car. There was a large window in the front of the car so she had a great view as the Skytrain left the airport.

Sumiko thought about her hand-map of Vancouver, to make sure the SkyTrain was going in the right direction. Sure enough, she was crossing from her index finger to the middle finger as the Skytrain rode a bridge over what must be the Fraser River. Confident that she was going in the right direction, Sumiko sat back and enjoyed the ride. At each station, a recorded voice called out the station name. Sumiko followed along by looking at the map displayed on the wall of her Skytrain car.

She was excited about the fact that she was being completely independent, having little difficulty finding her way to her homestay family.

An hour later, after finding her way to the train station just as the helpful girl at the airport had suggested, and Sumiko boarded the Via train for Edmonton.

It seemed strange to Sumiko that such a large train would be used to take people from downtown Vancouver to a little neighborhood in North Vancouver. And it was also strange that so many people had suitcases, as if they were going on a long trip.

It reminded her of a story David had told the English class, about his first days as a teacher in Kyoto. He said that he learned the hard way that if you are the only person sitting on a subway car in Japan, then get off, because the train is about to reverse direction. And he was right, when you are a stranger in a strange land, and you don't understand all the signs and the announcements at a train station, you have to be on the watch for things like that.

Once Sumiko found her seat and put her packsack in the overhead compartment, she took her ticket out of her travel pouch. She looked at it carefully. Yes, it said Edmonton. One way, $450. That seemed to be a bit expensive. Sumiko had paid for it using her Citibank Visa card and had thought nothing of the amount when she bought the ticket.

But now, something seemed wrong. The SkyTrain from the airport only cost $2.50, yet this train ride cost so much more. Why would it cost so much?

Feeling doubtful, Sumiko looked once again at the address of her homestay family. But she was interrupted by the sudden lurch as the train pulled out of the station.

She re-read the address and then she noticed that the address she wanted to go to was in North Vancouver, in an area called Edgemont Village. Yet her train ticket clearly said Edmonton, Alberta. Alberta? Wasn't that a completely different province than British Columbia?

Suddenly Sumiko began to worry that she was going in the completely wrong direction. As she continued reading her notes she noticed an even bigger problem. Her notes read: 'Meet homestay family at the arrivals terminal at Vancouver International Airport on 01 December. Call to confirm details any time on 01 November.'

Sumiko felt the blood flow from her face as her heart sunk in her chest. Oh no, what have I done? No wonder nobody was there to meet me, she thought to herself. I came one month too early! And instead of going to their home in Edgemont Village, in North Vancouver, I am on a train headed out of British Columbia, bound for Edmonton!

Distressed about her mistake, Sumiko waived her hand to get the attention of the friendly train conductor who had punched a hole in her ticket when the train first pulled out of the station.

"I am sorry. How does this journey take long?"

The conductor smiled at her as if she were his daughter and spoke slowly and very clearly. It was as if he knew that she was struggling with her English and that he had a lot of experience talking with foreigners. "It is written on the back of your ticket. Let's take a look together, shall we?" he said, reaching for her ticket. He turned it over and handed it back to her, pointing at the bottom line. "You see, 'Duration - 1 day, 1 hour and 30 minutes'. We left at six pm, and we will arrive in Edmonton at eight thirty tomorrow night."

Sumiko thought for a moment and frowned. "But that is one day, two hours and thirty minutes. Is my mash correct?"

Laughing in a nice way, the conductor explained "No, your math is correct but you did not add the extra hour for the time zone. Edmonton is in the Mountain Time Zone whereas Vancouver is in the Pacific Time Zone."

"Time Zone? What is that?"

"Where are you from, my dear?"

"I am from Kyoto. Where are you from?"

"I am from New Brunswick. But that's not the point. In your country, Japan, I think that there is only one time zone, right?"

"Oh, I understanding now. Yes, Japan Standard Time. How many time zones does Canada have?"

"We have six time zones."

"Wow. Is that because Canada is the biggest country in Earth?"

"Actually, Russia is much larger. They have nine time zones. But yes, it is because Canada is very large and the sun travels from the Atlantic side of the country first, at Newfoundland and Labrador, while we are still asleep out here in the west, and then makes its way across the country passing Alberta before setting west of British Columbia"

"It must be hard to remember these time zones."

"Not really, you just have to remember that the sun sets in the west, on its way to Japan!"

"Thank you!"

The conductor smiled at Sumiko before he continued down the aisle, resuming his duties.

Feeling much better after having had a real conversation with the nice man, Sumiko smiled to herself. She remembered something that her grandfather had told her. "When your life takes an unexpected turn, embrace it. You do not know where it will take you, but it will be your destiny," he had said.

Sumiko got out her journal and made the first journal entry of her adventure in Canada.

"01 November. Somehow I got the dates mixed up and flew to Canada one month too soon. I'm sure I told homestay Mama 'see you next month', but that was on 30 October. Maybe for

Canadians, next month does not mean one day later when it is a new month, November, but actually a whole month later, like 30 days. That could explain why she said 'call us again when you get closer to leaving'. That seemed strange at the time, but I did not say anything at the time. Anyhow, it turns out that I bought my ticket for one month too soon, so nobody was there to meet me at the airport. Then I got my homestay family's neighborhood in Edgemont Village mixed up, and now I am on a train journey to Edmonton, in Alberta! I have chosen to embrace this and follow it to wherever it takes me. I have one month to kill, after all. So I have decided to not contact my homestay family until later on in November. I'm on my own for now, so let the adventure in Alberta begin!"

After making her journal entry, Sumiko looked out the window at the farmland she was passing. Soon the farmland was replaced by forests, as enormous mountains grew larger and larger in the distance. She was headed into the Rocky Mountains! What beautiful scenery, she thought to herself, as she took out her digital camera to take some pictures.

9

HANDSOME STRANGER

The train journey to Edmonton was a wonderful trip for Sumiko. She spent hours and hours learning how to play a card game called 'cribbage' with some German backpackers and a couple from New Zealand. They spent hours together in a special train car that had huge curved windows that let her look up at the mountain peaks.

The mountains were majestic and Sumiko enjoyed every minute. She also made a great many mistakes in her English conversations with the Germans and the Kiwis but she did not care. They seemed to understand her and the Germans even made a few mistakes of their own. They all thought that Sumiko was very brave and adventurous for her decision to embrace the unknown, travelling to Edmonton on her own.

Once they arrived in Edmonton, Sumiko travelled with the Kiwis and stayed with them at a youth hostel. They explored the City of Edmonton together for a few days.

One of the best times they shared was a night in a O'Byrnes Irish Pub on Whyte Avenue. There was traditional Irish music and Sumiko got into a few conversations with complete strangers.

One of them helped to solve the mystery of how Sumiko had gotten so mixed up back at the Vancouver International Airport.

"You see, Sumiko, your homestay family live on Bonnie Doon court, in the Edgemont Village area, right?" He had asked. "And there is a Bonnie Doon neighborhood here in Edmonton. In fact, Bonnie Doon is only two kilometers from this very spot, further East along White Avenue. So it is completely understandable that on your first day in Canada, without any help at all, that you could have gotten it mixed up."

They all had a lot of fun laughing about it and everybody agreed that by spending a month on her own before the appointed time when she would meet her homestay family back in Vancouver, Sumiko would have a very memorable adventure.

After the Kiwis and Sumiko exchanged addresses and promised to keep in touch, Sumiko checked into the Fantasyland Hotel.

The hotel was luxurious and not nearly as expensive as a hotel in Japan would have been. It was located in the largest shopping mall she had ever seen, the West Edmonton Mall. The WEM itself had a pirate ship, submarines, a skating rink, a mini-golf course and a great many shops and restaurants. But what Sumiko liked most of all was the enormous waterslide park.

She spent a full week at the West Edmonton Mall and had some fun with some Japanese tourists from Tokyo. They told Sumiko about how much fun they had up in Yellowknife, and encouraged Sumiko to go there at some point. So Sumiko went to a travel agent in the shopping mall to enquire about tickets to Yellowknife.

Yellowknife is in the Arctic. But it is also not all that far from Edmonton because it was directly to the north of Edmonton. So she bought a return ticket for a four day trip and booked a room at the Explorer Hotel in Yellowknife.

When Sumiko got to the Edmonton International Airport she was very careful not to get confused again. It was actually quite easy to find her departure gate in the domestic terminal.

While she waited at the boarding gate, she saw that the aircraft had a polar bear painted on its tail. She saw another aircraft with what looked like a rainbow on it, but then she realized that it was actually the northern lights. It was the same airline as she had seen in David's photo album.

On the flight up to Yellowknife, the Captain informed the passengers that the northern lights could be seen out the right side windows. Sumiko had an aisle seat but there were some empty seats on the right side so she changed seats and stared out at the beautiful dancing lights in the night sky.

Once on the ground in Yellowknife Sumiko was surprised at how cold it was. It was minus thirty degrees Centigrade! It was so cold that her hands and face felt like they were freezing. But once she was settled into the Explorer Hotel she felt much better.

The next day she went across the street and found a small shopping center. She bought a few souvenirs, including some very warm fur boots and matching fur gloves, soapstone carvings and inukshuks.

She bought a carving of a dancing polar bear from some small community called Kimmirut, in Nunavut.

Now dressed more appropriately, Sumiko spent a day walking around the small city. She discovered a place called Tsunami Sushi, a small Japanese restaurant.

Inside, she felt at home. The menu was written in Japanese and English and the owners were actually from Japan. Most of the customers were local Yellowknife people. Sumiko listened to their conversations. A couple of really big men were talking about the new gold mine at some place called the Tyhee Gold Mine. Gold mining seemed to be on everybody's lips, and also part of the history of the community.

Sumiko thought it was funny, seeing these giant men with somewhat dirty hands eating tiny Sushi morsels. It made her start to like these hard-working types of people she seemed to see everywhere in Yellowknife. She also talked with a few Japanese people. But something was beginning to bother her.

It had first started in Edmonton, when she had linked up with that group of Japanese tourists, and she felt that it was happening again. Sumiko was talking a lot more in Japanese than in English. It felt like a trap.

With so many Japanese tourists visiting Canada, Sumiko had found it relatively easy to find other Japanese people to strike up conversations with. But whenever she hung out with Japanese people she would invariably find that they did not want to actually talk in English. This seemed to be limiting her own opportunity to fully immerse in English. So the next day, Sumiko went out on her own.

She took a taxi to the far side of Yellowknife, to take a dogsled ride from the most famous dogsled family in town, the Beck family. When she got there, a large group of American tourists were just leaving. They seemed very happy after their dogsled ride.

Sumiko talked with Patrick Beck, the dog handler that was going to take her out. But he said that she had to wait because he had to take care of the two dog teams that had just finished taking the Americans out. Sumiko did not mind. She hung around Patrick as he fed and un-harnessed his dogs. She did not try to initiate any conversation with Patrick, but Sumiko really enjoyed being around the excited dogs as they yelped and jumped around. They were so energetic!

Finally the time came for her dogsled ride. She sat in the back of the dogsled. There was lots of empty space in front of her in the big dogsled. Patrick was behind her, standing on the skis and holding the dogsled reigns and calling out sharp commands to team of eight dogs, in pairs of two.

It was a sunny and windless day. The sky was an incredibly deep shade of blue. The air felt crisp and fresh and her fur gloves and insulated boots kept her warm as the sled whooshed along the trail from the Beck property.

Soon they were out on a lake with the dogs running for all that they were worth. They seemed to love running and pulling the dogsled. And then Sumiko saw the most ridiculous thing she had ever seen.

One after another, it seemed, each of the dogs had to have a poop. But running so fast as they were they could not stop to do their business. The dogs had to somehow double-jump their hind legs so that they could poop on the run. It looked incredibly awkward, but when you have to go, you have to go, she guessed. Then the smell would waft back and hit her. It was unpleasant for a moment and then the smell was instantly replaced by cold, fresh air again.

Sumiko was not sure whether this disgusted her or intrigued her more. She decided that there was nothing wrong with it. That's just what it is like to ride in a dogsled in the Canadian Arctic. So she embraced it as just part of the experience.

Soon her face began to feel very cold, even though she was wearing a very thick winter coat provided by Mr. Beck. So when Patrick made the dogs stop, she was relieved to have the wind stop, allowing her to warm her face up a bit. She watched as Patrick waived his arms at someone coming out of the forest.

A tall man wearing some kind of orange snow-suit was plodding through very deep snow. Sumiko imagined that it must be very hard to walk in such deep snow, and wondered why he did not have snow shoes or cross-country skis.

Soon enough she understood why he did not, as she listened to his conversation with Patrick.

"I'm so glad you stopped! My sled broke down about 2k's back there," said the young man. "I was afraid I would have to walk all the way out! Will you give me ride back to your place?" He said.

"Sure. Climb in there behind my customer, I have to keep the weight to the back on this sled," said Patrick.

Sumiko was having a hard time understanding the conversation. If the man's sled was broken, what happened to his dogs? She wondered, as she slid forward to make room for him in the dogsled.

The man smiled at her as he stepped over the rail and climbed into the rear of the dogsled, immediately behind Sumiko.

He was so handsome, she thought to herself. He had whiskers on his face, a perfect nose, and the deepest blue eyes she had ever seen.

With little room for his large arms between the rails of the sled, the only place he could put his arms was around Sumiko's waist. He slid his hands around her thin waist in a casual manner, as though it was completely natural.

For Sumiko it was decidedly not casual. His strong hands around her body made her shiver with goose bumps. The warm air of his breath made a silver cloud of fog with each breath, which rolled past her right side. It hung in the air near her right cheek like a soft kiss. When she drew in a breath she could taste his breath in the air.

As the dogsled raced back across the lake to the Beck property, Sumiko could not help but to relax and lean back into his warmth. She felt so comfortable and cozy, nestled as she was in his lap. But she could not turn to look at him. Not only because there was no room for such a twist, but also because she was intensely nervous, afraid to do anything.

Once the dogsled pulled up at the Beck property and she was helped out of it by Patrick, Sumiko hoped to have a conversation with the handsome stranger. But for some reason, probably because of how aroused she was feeling after riding in the strangers lap for the last fifteen minutes, Sumiko could not utter a word.

The stranger smiled at her again. His face was burned into her memory like a great work of art. His smile seemed to hang in the air as it transfixed Sumiko, motionless in her excitement.

"Thanks, Pat. I'll make it up to you!" the man said, and then he promptly waived goodbye to Sumiko as he began to jog away up the road.

All that Sumiko could do was to wave goodbye to the handsome man.

Later that night, in her room at the Explorer Hotel, Sumiko was awake well into the middle of the night, uselessly thinking of all the things she could have said to the handsome stranger. At the very least she should have asked him for his name. But his presence had been so powerful that Sumiko had been petrified. She knew that what she had experienced was that rare, unforgettable event in one's life—love at first sight.

She also knew that because of her sudden inability to speak, it would also be unrequited love.

10

NELSON

Sumiko was just completing yet another journal entry when she was interrupted.

"You're spending more time writing in your book than you are looking out the window," said the middle-aged woman standing in the aisle.

Sumiko had been riding on the Greyhound bus for nearly ten hours and was becoming extremely tired, so the sudden interruption caught her off guard.

"Excuse me?" stammered Sumiko, putting her journal into her packsack and turning her full attention to the woman.

"You are missing some beautiful scenery, look at that skyline!" the woman said.

Sumiko looked out at the bright blue background and the magnificent mountains outside the bus window.

"Yes, it is truly wonderful. I love it, and would like to watch it all, but I am making notes about everything I just saw in Banff," said Sumiko.

"How long were you in Banff?"

"As long as the bus, maybe 30 minutes."

"Oh, I thought you had just got on the bus there. So you really didn't see much of Banff at all?"

"That's right. It looks like the perfect place to spend a week or even longer. So much natural beauty, so many things to see," beamed Sumiko.

"Where did you get on the bus?"

"In Edmonton, early this morning."

"That would make for a long day. Did you know that you were getting on the 'milk run'?"

"What means 'milk run?'" asked Sumiko

"It's a bus route that stops in each and every crappy little town along the way. Sort of the opposite of an express bus."

Laughing, Sumiko understood. "Like a milk delivery truck, stopping at each house! Yes, this has been a real milking run. But I am really enjoying it. I have taken a lot of pictures, especially in Jasper and at that glacier we stopped at before Lake Louise."

"So where are you headed to?"

"I am on my way back to Vancouver. I guess we will get there tomorrow afternoon. I hope I can get some sleep on the bus, but it's starting to get a little uncomfortable. Maybe the express bus would have been better."

"Yeah, you would have arrived in Vancouver by now, actually. I missed the express bus myself, but I like stopping in the small towns along the way, really brings back memories."

"Why? Were you a bus driver?"

"No. I lived in the Rockies when I was a young girl. Now I live in Toronto. I'm on my way to Creston to see my sister and her kids – my nieces."

"Where is Creston?"

"It's right after Nelson. We should be arriving in Nelson in a few hours. Actually, you will have over an hour to kill in Nelson, according to the bus schedule," she said.

"Really. What is there to do in Nelson at this late hour?"

"Take a walk along Baker Street. There are some beautiful historic buildings dating back to the 1890's."

"Is that old? In Japan, where I am from, 100 years is not really considered to be all that old," Sumiko said, with pride.

"Well, in Canada, a century is a very long time. Don't forget, we just became a country in 1867."

"What was Canada before that?"

"We were a colony of England. But in 1867 all of the British Colonies in North American were united by the British North America Act, which created the Dominion of Canada. Of course, some parts of Canada were actually part of France, you know, but came under British rule after the defeat of France in the Battle of the Plains of Abraham. Or actually, maybe it was a few years after that. Anyhow, the point is that Canadian history is both French and British."

"Oh yes, I read that about Canada. That's why you have English and French as two official languages!" said Sumiko.

"Well, you know a lot about Canada. But did you know that most of the original buildings in Nelson, and also Vancouver for that matter, were destroyed by fire?

We used to build our buildings out of wood, but time after time a house fire would spread and destroy the town. So over in Nelson they got sick of rebuilding again and again. After they made a law that new buildings had to be built out of stone, in about 1890, the town stopped burning down. In Vancouver, the entire town was burned to the ground in 1886. Of course, back then, the town was very small, mostly around what we call Gastown today. Have you seen 'Gassy Jack'?" asked the lady

"Gassy Jack? No. Who is he?"

"There is a statue of him standing on a whiskey barrel, in Gastown. His name was Captain Gassy Jack Deighton, 'gassy' not because of passing wind, but because he was a great orator."

"Wind? Orator? I don't understand."

"Gassy could mean farting, passing wind. But it also means 'full of hot air', or talking a lot," she explained.

"I understand, someone who talks a lot makes a lot of wind. Like a gas. But not like a.." Sumiko smiled, a bit embarrassed, but since there was nobody else sitting nearby she went ahead and said the crude word, "fart!"

"Yeah, lots of people laugh at his name, thinking it's about farting. Anyhow, he was the founding father of Vancouver. He owned a bar in New Westminster and decided to open a saloon near the forestry workers who were cutting trees where Vancouver is now. There was no city or town there at that time, so he travelled down river from New Westminster with a keg of whiskey in his boat. When he got to where the logging was happening, he set up a tent as his saloon and started selling whiskey. That enterprise led to more permanent structures and a settlement called 'Granville', which Capt. Gassy Jack mostly owned. That's why Granville Street is one of the main streets in Vancouver, and why the historic part of the town is called Gastown. I think that was in 1867. I'm surprised you have never heard of it, and haven't been there yet. There is also an amazing musical steam-driven mechanical clock in Gastown that everybody takes pictures of"

"I have not seen Vancouver yet," said Sumiko.

"But I thought you said you were going *back* to Vancouver?"

"I am. But I was only there for a few minutes, to get on the train to Edmonton."

"Oh, I see. So you really haven't seen much of the city at all, then?"

"No, but I am going to live there, so I will explore it every day. I think I will look for Captain Jack on one of my first days! He sounds like a real pioneer." A thoughtful look came across Sumiko's face. She was pretty sure that she had understood most of what the woman had told her, and then she made a connection.

"Did you say that Gassy Jack started Vancouver in 1867?"

"Yeah, I think that was when it was."

"And you also said that the Dominion of Canada, as its own country, started in 1867?"

"Yes, that's right."

"I don't understand. So Canada becomes a country when places like Vancouver are still not even towns? How can that be? Where were all the people living?"

"Well, you have to understand, most of the action was in Eastern Canada and the Maritimes, the east coast. Nothing much was happening out here on the west coast of Canada. In fact, even in the US, places like Los Angeles – all of California in fact – was still part of Mexico until it was given by Mexico to the US in 1848, after the Mexican American War. So all of the west coast of North American was basically new territories for the US and for England, while the east coast had been settled and developed into communities for almost two hundred years by that time," explained the lady.

"So why was North America settled on the East coast first?"

"Because that side, where Halifax, New York, Charlottetown, and the like are located, is just across the Atlantic ocean from England. To get to British Columbia or to California, from England, you had to sail all around the world!"

Sumiko thought about this for a few minutes. trying to get a handle on the complicated history of Canada, and then she had an insight. "So that is why the railroad being completed, through Edmonton and Jasper and then on to BC, was so important? To take people to the west from the east?" asked Sumiko.

"Yes, the railroad helped build Canada, after it had become a nation in 1867."

"Yes, I remember reading that the last spike in the railroad, completing the construction of the first rail link all the way across the continent, was in 1885. But where was that done, I forget?"

"Near Revelstoke, here in BC," said the lady.

"Does this bus go to Revelstoke?"

"No that's a bit north of here. But there is so much to see and do in Nelson. And here we are!

We are arriving in Nelson. I'm changing buses here, and I think I see them loading passengers on my bus, so I can't show you around Nelson, sorry. But it sure was nice talking to you!"

"It was nice talking with you, too! Enjoy your visit with your sisters and your cousins!"

"Nieces. Not cousins. The children of my sister, the girls, they are my nieces, not cousins!"

"Oh, I'm sorry. Thanks for correcting my terrible English." Sumiko was a little embarrassed.

"Not at all! Your English is coming along very well. Don't' be afraid to make a few little mistakes, just keep on talking. You're doing great. Bye-bye!!" she waived, getting off the bus as soon as the door was opened.

Sumiko smiled as she watched the lady rush to the other bus and climb on board. Some people in Canada seem to be so nice and friendly, thought Sumiko, for perhaps the twentieth time on her trip so far.

Her reflections were suddenly interrupted as the bus driver stood up to address the remaining passengers.

"Ladies and Gentlemen, we have arrived in Nelson. I have some good news and some bad news. The bad news is that our bus is no longer serviceable. There is a problem with the electrical system and we have to stay here in Nelson until some time tomorrow before a replacement bus will arrive."

Sumiko was a bit confused, but thought that she understood that there would be an overnight delay. For a moment she was concerned that she would not know what to do, where to go, or where to stay. But then she thought about something her father had told her before she set off on her adventure in Canada. "Embrace life, make friends, and do not be afraid. The universe will provide whatever you need," he had said.

And then her positive attitude was immediately rewarded.

"And what's the good news?" asked one of the passenger, sounding angry.

"The Greyhound company has arranged for your overnight accommodations," he said with a smile.'

"Where are we staying?" asked another passengcr.

"Well, that's why it's good news. The cheap hotels downtown are all booked up, so you are – we are all – being put up in a resort! It's called 'Ainsworth Hot Springs Resort". It's about twenty kilometers along the far side of Kootenay Lake from here. You all get a hotel room, dinner, breakfast, and free access to the hot springs!"

said the bus driver, clearly enjoying delivering the good news.

Without exception, all the passengers suddenly cheered up. A free night in a spa resort, meals included, that sure beat sitting on the bus for another 14 hours.

Within 30 minutes, Sumiko and the other passengers arrived at Ainsworth Hot Springs. None of the other passengers seemed interesting to Sumiko, so she basically stayed to herself. Hanging back to observe what was said when each person checked in at the registration desk, Sumiko was the last person to check in.

"Greyhound?" asked the tired looking clerk.

"Yes, Greyhound," said Sumko.

"Fill out your name and sign at the bottom. I'll fill out the rest. Here is your room key. You've got about thirty minutes before the kitchen closes, so you'd better hustle your buns," she said.

"Thank you!" said Sumiko, thinking that she would have to look up what 'hustle your buns' meant. She was pretty sure it would not be in her Japanese – English dictionary.

By the time she found her room on the third floor she had figured out what hustle your buns meant, and knew that she had to hurry. So she simply tossed her backpack on one of the two large beds in her suite and rushed to the restaurant before it was too late to get dinner. She hustled her buns.

An hour later, after enjoying the buffet style dinner and a few tasty dessert treats, Sumiko had changed into her swimsuit and headed down to the pool.

The pool at Ainsworth Hot Springs had once been very nice, but seemed to have fallen into disrepair over the years. To Sumiko, it was not as well maintained or as clean as a Japanese onsen. The contrast between Japan and Canada was a bit of a shock to Sumiko. Whereas in Japan, people would spend twenty minutes or longer washing and cleaning themselves before entering a pool or other public bathing place, there was no such tradition of cleanliness in Canada. There was a sign in the changing room that read: "Shower before entering the pool", but it was obvious to Sumiko that most of the other bathers did not even bother to have a shower, let alone to wash themselves properly with a cloth and soap.

At first she found it disgusting, and considered not even going into the water. However, as Sumiko walked out to the pool area after carefully washing herself in the Japanese manner, she was immediately impressed by how clean and clear the water in the pool looked. That, and thoughts of her father's advice about embracing life in Canada without being judgmental, and Sumiko decided to take the plunge and enter the water.

The waters of the pool were warm, but certainly not a hot spring. Sumiko waded around in the large pool, looking out over Kootenay Lake as she took in her surroundings. And then she saw the cave. People were coming out of a hole in the rock, adjacent to the pool. That must be where the hot spring is, thought Sumiko.

She got out of the pool and headed up the steps towards the cave entrance when she heard a scream.

A young woman was being pushed into the water of a very small pool, just beside the cave entrance. After being momentarily frightened, Sumiko realize that the woman was only screaming because the water she had been shoved into was extremely cold. That was something she had seen many times in Japan, a cold bath next to a hot one, so you could experience both extremes.

The cold pool had a waterfall under which the young couple were now playfully embracing each other in a public display of affection which Sumiko admired. That sort of thing was rarely seen in Japan, but Sumiko considered herself to be the sort of person who, if in love, would be uninhibited about embracing or even kissing her lover in public.

The hot water of the cave pool was mild by Japanese standards but as she waded deeper into the cave, and as the water of the wading pool/tunnel became deeper, the water became hotter. It was clear to Sumiko that at some point deep in the cave there was an actual hot spring where geo-thermally heated water from deep in the earth was gushing out into the cave.

As she relaxed in the heat of the pool, Sumiko thought again of the young couple she had seen frolicking in the cold pool. Her mind drifted away to a daydream about how it would be to be in the arms of the tall, handsome stranger who had been haunting her thoughts ever since he cast his deep blue eyes on her in Yellowknife. These thoughts, and the increasing heat of the cave, made her happy that the cave was very dark, lit only by the yellow lights strung along the ceiling of the cave and a few underwater lights along the floor.

She was certain that her cheeks were very red. She would have felt a bit embarrassed at her arousal if she had been in the light of day.

As it was, here in the cave, she felt relaxed. It even felt a bit romantic to her, thinking of the lover that could have been, while being safely anonymous in the cave. So she lingered in the cave, letting other people pass her by as they walked through the horse-shoe shaped tunnel.

At the farthest end of the tunnel, Sumiko found a place where the side of the cave opened up and sloped uphill, into a nook that was shaped like a large horn. A man had been sitting there moments before and had just climbed down from the nook and got back into the water and walked out of the cave. This made the natural sauna of the nook available to Sumiko.

She climbed up into the nook and found a comfortable rock to sit on. Pulling her knees up to her chest, she wrapped her arms around her legs and leaned her face onto her knees and closed her eyes.

There, in the intense heat of the nook, with her eyes closed, Sumiko relaxed into a meditative state. Without concentrating or even directing her thoughts she recalled the man's face as clear as if she were looking at him. His unshaven face was rugged, with that cinnamon colored skin a man gets if he is exposed to wind and sun. The sort of real man that Sumiko knew she would one day find, the sort of man she had found and then lost.

After a few minutes in the heat of the nook fantasizing about the man of her dreams, Sumiko was ready to take the plunge. With a smile on her face, thinking about the two meanings of 'take the plunge', Sumiko jumped into the cold pool and let out a hearty 'whoooh!' when she came back up to the surface. She was absolutely refreshed by the plunge into the cold water.

An hour later, after getting dressed and having a bottle of Kokanee beer at the hotel bar, Sumiko headed up to her room. She called room service and ordered another bottle of Kokanee to enjoy in her room. On the label of the very good tasting beer, she read: 'Brewed Right, in the Kootenays'. Feeling very fine after a sauna and two beers, she decided right then and there that Kokanee was her favorite beer in Canada.

She turned on the hotel TV to see what the local television station had to offer and was surprised to see that a movie was just starting to play.

As she would later learn, the main channel of the hotel television system had a continuous loop with the same movie playing again and again. The movie was a lot of fun. It was about a man with an enormous nose. He falls in love with a beautiful young woman. The man was older than the young woman and he had to compete with a younger man, a handsome fireman, for the woman's affections. As Sumiko watched the romantic comedy, starring Steve Martin, she had a strange feeling about the movie. It was set in a mountainous city with lots of beautiful stone buildings.

And then she figured it out, just by reading a few of the signs on buildings and on the fire truck: 'Nelson Fire Department', the movie was set in Nelson! No wonder the hotel had it playing continuously on one of the channels, it really made you want to spend more time in Nelson.

The next day, with several hours to spend after breakfast, waiting for the bus departure time, Sumiko walked all around the beautiful and historic town. She bought a few souvenirs and tried to figure out which restaurant was the one featured in the movie. She found the Nelson Fire Hall and the house where the romance had taken place. It was a real adventure for her, and felt very romantic to Sumiko. But soon enough her time in Nelson was over and it was time to get on the new bus and resume her long bus journey to home to Vancouver.

11

SPUZZUM IS BEYOND HOPE

Only 8 hours later the bus arrived in Vancouver. Unlike the first bus, this new bus was not a milk run. It was an express bus, so there were few stops. This gave Sumiko more time to update her journal and to write letters to her sister, parents and friends. By the time the bus pulled into the terminal in downtown Vancouver Sumiko had about a dozen post-cards ready to mail.

The first conversation she had on the bus had been a few hours before arriving in Vancouver, just as the bus descended out of the mountains before reaching the start of the Fraser Valley. She had talked with a strange young man who had been sitting beside her. He told her about the Jericho Beach Youth Hostel. From what he had said, she could check in there for up to three nights and spend her days exploring the beaches and parks of Vancouver's west side. All she had to do was find a bus to the end of the middle finger, to Jericho Beach.

Just before the young man got off the bus, Sumiko tried to read his T-shirt.

"What means, 'Heck' and 'Spuzzoom'?"

Looking down at his T-Shirt, "Oh, you mean my T-shirt? It says, 'Where the heck is Spuzzum?' I got this from my cousin in Spuzzum. It's a joke. 'Where the heck is Spuzzum?' means where in the world is Spuzzum?' and the answer is 'Spuzzum is beyond Hope,'" he said with a smile. Then he suddenly got up and grabbed his bag.

"And here we are. Spuzzum. If you blink, you'll miss it. Nice talking to you. Bye Bye!"

As she watched the strange boy get off the bus and cross the street, Sumiko was trying to understand what was funny about his joke. The town of Spuzzum itself looked like it was no more than a coffee shop and a few ramshackle houses. It almost had a hopeless feeling to it, she thought to herself. Maybe that's what 'beyond hope' means.

She thought no more of it until about an hour later when the bus pulled into a much larger town. Sumiko noticed that the landscape was suddenly changing from high mountains and deep valleys to what must be the start of a valley. She could see in the skyline to the west that there were no more mountains. She was about to look at her map to figure out where she was when she noticed a sign at the side of the road: 'Welcome to Hope. Population 6,809.'

Sumiko laughed out loud, which was unusual for her, but she could not help herself. She finally got it, she understood the joke. She understood that there were two meanings. 'Beyond hope' means past the town called 'Hope', on the highway, but it also means has that the town of Spuzzum is so small and insignificant that it has no more hope, no chance for good things to happen! It truly is hopeless, or 'beyond hope'. When Sumiko finally understood the joke, she laughed out loud. When other passengers looked at her strangely, she only laughed harder. It became contagious, making others begin to laugh without even having a reason. Eventually she calmed down and another passenger got up out of her seat and walked along the aisle to ask Sumiko "I just have to ask, what was so funny?"

Sumiko began to answer with a straight face, but only got out a few words, "Spuzzum is beyond..." and then burst out laughing again, almost hysterically.

"Oh yeah, I get it, 'Spuzzum is beyond Hope'. I heard that freaky young man telling you that joke about an hour ago. Did you really only just get the joke now?"

"Yes. I understand why he was funny now."

"Priceless!" the lady said, smiling.

"Priceless?"

"Yes, your getting the joke so long after it was spoken, that is great fun, it is priceless," she said, sitting down next to Sumiko. "So where are you traveling to and from?"

"To? From? Oh, I understand. I am travelling from Japan. I am going to" Sumiko had to think about that for a moment, then she showed the woman her right hand and pointed to the middle finger. "I am going here, to the youth hotel on this beach!"

The woman's face knotted up in concentration.

"You better be careful with that middle finger. You know what it means, don't you?"

"Yes. It is the middle part of the city, where the University is, here, on the finger nail. And this finger is downtown, with Stanley Park on the finger nail. And this little finger is the North Mountains, where Goose Mountain rights up the sky at night," explained Sumiko.

"Oh, I see. Yes, I never looked at it that way. What a great way to explain where things are in the city. Did you think of that all by yourself?"

"No. My English Teacher at the International Center, David, taught it to me. I thing it working good, yes?"

"Yes, I think you are right, it really does work well. You seem to know Vancouver like the back of your hand! But if you stick up that middle finger by itself, someone might be offended."

"You mean 'Fuck You?' I know that, we have that gesture in Japan now too."

The lady and Sumiko laughed at that together.

"How long have you been in Vancouver, and where were you yesterday?"

"I was in Edmonton and in Yellowknife, and spent last night in Nelson. I had such a great experiences and fun! But I have not really seen any of Vancouver yet. I saw the city from the air when I arrived from Japan. Then I took the SkyTrain to the Via train, and went to Edmonton. So I am just now starting my trip in Vancouver," explained Sumiko. But I do know one thing, I want to see Gassy Jack's statue first thing, maybe even today!" she said.

"Well, young lady, you sure seem to have a good sense of directions, and your English is very good. You've got your head on your shoulders."

"Thank you! Can you really understand me good?"

"Yes, I can really understand you well. So how did you learn so much English? Did you study a lot in Japan?"

"No. Not really. I had read a lot of books and taken some conversational classes, but my learning has been much faster now that I am here. Canadian people are easy to talk to so I am getting into conversations very many times. That is helping me push my English"

"Really? That's great." After a short pause the lady smiled playfully at Sumiko, and continued. "And while you have been 'pushing' your English, have you had any conversations with any handsome young men?"

Sumiko's face reddened and her smile faded. "Yes, I have talked to one beautiful man," and then Sumiko seemed to shut down and not want to talk any more, looking crushed.

The woman thought that she understood. "It did not go well with your handsome man, I can see. I am sorry to hear that. Did he hurt you?"

"Hurt me? No, of course not. He was very nice."

"So why the long face?"

"Long face? Oh, yes, my sad face must be very ugly, I am sorry." Sumiko covered her face with her hands and tried to hide. The woman stayed silent, looking away from Sumiko to give her some space.

Then Sumiko felt stupid. She felt stupid for not asking the man in Yellowknife for his name, for not even trying to have a real conversation with him, for not having his email address. She felt even more stupid for behaving like a shy Japanese wall-flower, hiding her face behind her hands. In the nearly four weeks since she had arrived in Vancouver, Sumiko had behaved more and more like a Canadian girl, not hiding her face behind her hands but opening her face and her life to life itself. Now, suddenly, with her long sad face and shame for the lost chance at love, she is afraid again? This is not acceptable, thought Sumiko.

"Actually, it is very romantic, like Shakespeare," said Sumiko, taking her hands away from her face and making an effort to smile.

"Shakespeare? How so? You mean tragic?"

"Yes! Tragic but romantic. How do you say it in English, Not realized love?"

"Unrequited love. Exactly. And you have no way to find this man again?"

"No way. He is in Yellowknife and I do not know anything about him. I too afraid asking him to seat in a coffee and have a cap of coffee."

"You were too shy to invite him to a café for a cup of coffee? Well, my dear, you are a beautiful and spirited young girl. You will find your love one day. Who knows, it could be just around the corner. Life has a way of opening a door when it closes a window. So forget about what cannot be and enjoy whatever comes next! That's the way to be."

These words restored Sumiko's spirit and made her eager to see what new adventure she was going to find.

That one of her adventures would put her life in danger was the farthest thing from her mind.

12

MIDDLE FINGER

As the bus finally pulled into the terminal, Sumiko recognized where she was. The Greyhound Bus terminal was at the same place where she had boarded the Via train just two weeks before. Sumiko was suddenly very excited that she would start her first full day in Vancouver at a place she understood.

Getting off of the bus, she read "Pacific Central Station, Vancouver's Hub for Bus and Train Travel." Then she remembered something she had read in a travel magazine and realized that she must be very close to some interesting things, but Sumiko could not remember what they were.

Her pack felt light on her back as she set off walking out of the station, eager to find out where she was. Sure enough, within a few minutes she had located a billboard with a city map. After finding the "You Are Here" marked on the map, she compared the map to the back of her right hand. After getting her bearings, she was certain that she was at the junction between her ring finger and her middle finger. So she must be close to the body of water that separates downtown from the next peninsula of land jutting out into the water, she thought to herself.

After turning to her right to confirm her sense of direction, Sumiko was so happy to see the mountains in the distance to the north. They looked different than when she had first arrived. They now had a beautiful frosting of white snow on the higher reaches of the mountains, and the lush green of the forests below. The mountains to the north had become her friends because they helped Sumiko know where she was at all times.

She looked at the billboard map again, and found that Pacific Central Station was right next to the SkyTrain station. She remembered coming out of that very SkyTrain station almost a month before. That memory did not interest her as much as seeing that she was just a few hundred metres from Science World and the end of False Creek, something new to explore!

Sumiko walked away from the station, passed the stairs leading up to the SkyTrain, and continued on to cross Main Street.

The pedestrian 'Walk' – 'Don't Walk' signal at the street corner was funny to look at for Sumiko. She soon understood that a red hand, her map of the city, meant: 'Don't Walk', and a white outline of a person walking meant 'Walk'.

As she hurried across the wide street Sumiko looked ahead and saw the beautiful silver geodesic dome of Telus Science World, and the headwaters of False Creek beyond.

When she got to the Science World, she did not enter. She just walked up to the railing at one side and looked out over the water. She could see on her right, heading out her ring finger so to speak, the cluster of tall buildings of downtown Vancouver.

On the left, heading up her middle finger, was a ridge that ran as far as the eye could see. It was completely covered with short buildings that were obviously condominiums.

Between these two peninsulas was False Creek. Sumiko looked out over the water at the beautiful yachts in small groups at a number of exclusive marinas on either side of False Creek.

Peering off into the distance and peeking under a large bridge, by squinting her eyes Sumiko could see yet another bridge linking downtown with the main residential core of the city, the West

End. No, Sumiko corrected herself, the West Side. The *West End* is a different area, near Stanley Park while the *West Side* is an entirely different peninsula, and where she wanted to go today.

So without any idea of how she would get there, Sumiko turned to her left and began walking along a beautiful walkway on the south side of False Creek.

It all looked new, as though the entire area had just been built. Sumiko was very impressed. She wondered if all of the city was in such perfect condition.

After walking for just a few minutes, Sumiko passed over a very short and unusual bridge. It must have cost a fortune, judging by the interesting architecture of the short span footbridge. A short distance later, Sumiko found a tiny island just a few meters from the shoreline. Obviously man-made, the island looked like an attempt to give back to nature, a small piece of sanctuary for birds and other creatures. There were some comfortable looking benches nearby, so she sat down to listen to the sounds of the birds, to feel the wind blowing in her hair, and just to get to know this interesting little spot she had discovered.

From where she sat, Sumiko was looking to the north, with the apartment buildings and office towers reaching up to the sky on the other side of False Creek and the snow-frosted mountains beyond. There was a big stadium with a white roof, which Sumiko recognized as the BC Place football stadium, and a small marina with some very expensive looking yachts.

It was a beautiful, sunny winter's day. Not at all the rainy, grey sky that some people had told her about Vancouver in the winter.

Just then a lady walking her dog came by and sat down on the bench beside Sumiko. The little dog started yelping excitedly and sniffing at Sumiko's leg.

"Now, Bella, don't bother the nice lady, Sit still!" She said to her doggie.

"Oh, that's OK, I like dogs!" said Sumiko.

"Bella is not a dog," said the lady, "or at least, not in her mind. She is a little prima donna! Aren't you, my little princess!"

"What breeding her?"

"What breed is she? She's a Multi-Poodle."

"She is very friendliness. I like her!" Sumiko said, reaching down to play with the dog. Sumiko felt comfortable and relaxed, and in no hurry to go anywhere.

"Do you and Bella live near here?"

"Oh no! We live up on Fourth Avenue. We like to walk along the waterfront here, the mornings. We start out here at the Olympic Village, and walk all the way to Granville Island, and then back," said the elderly lady.

"I have heard about Granville Island. Is it far?"

"From here? It's about 3 kilometers, maybe less. About a 45 minute walk along the creek."

"Why did you call this place the Athlete's Village? Do football players live here?"

"Football players? Why would they live here?"

"Isn't that the football stadium, over there? And they are athletes," reasoned Sumiko.

"Oh yeah, I see your logic. But no. At least, probably not. There could be football players here, but it's called 'Athlete's Village' because it was built for the Vancouver 2010 Games," she said.

"Oh! I understand. That makes sense now. That is why all of this is new. So it's not nice and new like this everywhere in the city?"

"It varies. The False Creek area, all along this body of water in front of us, has been built up over the years ever since about 1986, when we had Expo 1986 here in Vancouver. You see that glassy rooftop area over there?" she said, pointing to the area right across from where they sat, and near the football stadium.

"Yes, it looks a bit older than where we are."

"That's right. That's the 'Plaza of Nations'. I think there is a casino and a few bars there now, but that all dates back to '86, you know, 'Expo 86?' Anyhow, past that, down to our left, along the way to Granville Island, there are lots of condos and apartments from the '80's and '90's, a really interesting variety of architectural styles. Are you walking that way?"

Her head almost spinning from the old lady's rambling explanation, Sumiko tried to keep up. "Yes, I guess," said Sumiko, "I'm just working my way that way to Jericho Beach. How long will it take to walk there?"

"I guess you could walk it, but it would take hours and hours. You would be better off taking the bus up on Fourth Avenue."

"Thanks. I think I will walk to Granville Island first. There is a grocery store there, I think."

"Grocery store? There's a whole lot more than that! There's a wonderful farmer's marketplace there. All sorts of fruits, meats, bakeries, art shops, restaurants and tourist shops. You could spend your entire day on Granville Island. Bella and I are walking that way, would you like to walk with us?"

Sumiko and the old woman talked all the way to Granville Island. It turned out that Doris had even been to Kyoto on a conference trip years ago, when she was a University Professor. She had forgotten all of her Japanese words over the years, and made Sumiko help her remember a few Japanese words. By the end of their walk together, Sumiko had learned a lot about the history of the False Creek area and planned to come back and explore it in the future.

By the time they reached Granville Island, Sumiko realized that she should skip it for the day and focus on getting to the Jericho Beach Youth Hostel. After saying thank you to Doris and bye-bye to Bella, Sumiko followed the road up under the Granville Street Bridge towards Fourth Avenue, just as Doris had directed her to do.

Finding the bus stop was not difficult. All Sumiko had to do was look at each and every road-side sign along the westbound side of the road and figure out what each sign meant.

It was something of a game to Sumiko. Some of the signs made no sense at all. They must have had something to do with when you could park and when you could not park your car along the side of the road. Eventually she found what must be a bus stop, where other people were standing around waiting. With no idea which bus to take, Sumiko just observed what other people were doing, and watched the cars driving by.

The cars themselves were very different from cars in Japan. They were much larger and there were some very fancy looking cars. When one extremely long car, a limousine, passed by, Sumiko began to think about how Vancouver was known as 'Hollywood North' for all the movies filmed in Vancouver. She imagined for a moment that the limousine could have a real life movie star in it, perhaps even Vancouver-born actor, Ryan Reynolds, her favorite movie star.

The sudden arrival of a bus broke Sumiko out of her thoughts. Saying to herself in Japanese, 'dozo, osakini' she simply put out her hand as a gesture as she let the other passengers get on the bus ahead of her, Sumiko tried to figure out how to pay for a bus ride. It wasn't until after all the other passengers had passed her that she remembered how to say: "after you". Watching them boarding the bus, she saw people showing some sort of identity pass or maybe a bus ticket to the bus driver, and then one person put some coins into a funny machine at the front of the bus, right beside the bus driver.

"Excuse me. How much coins?" she asked, not sure if she had formed the question correctly but also not all that worried about it. If she got it wrong then she would have collected another mistake and therefore have learned something.

"How many coins, for the bus fare?" asked the driver as he pulled the bus out into traffic. "For how many zones?"

"I don't know how many zones. I am going to Jericho Beach."

"Oh. That's just one zone. Two Fifty."

"Two Dollars and Fifty Cents?"

"Yes. Just put the money in there."

Sumiko took out a toonie and two quarters. By now she was very familiar with Canadian coins. Her favorite was the toonie, because it had a Polar bear on it and that reminded her of her short trip to Yellowknife and the handsome man she had met, fallen for, and then lost.

She put the money into the machine and the machine pushed out a paper card with a time stamp on it.

"What is this for?"

"It's called a 'Transfer'. You see the numbers on the bottom? That tells you what time the transfer card expires. Before that time you can use it to get on another bus in the same zone and continue travelling without paying again," he explained. Just stick it into the box on your next bus, and the ride is free!"

"Oh, that's good! I like that!" Sumiko said, genuinely happy to know how to save money. "Thank you for the Transfer!" she said. The bus driver smiled warmly at her, as though she had been more polite than was necessary.

After riding on the bus for about twenty minutes, watching out the window for any signs for Jericho Beach, Sumiko began to worry if she had missed her stop. She was certain that the water was several blocks to the north, away from Fourth Avenue, but she did not know how the streets or numbers worked in Vancouver. So she stood up and moved closer to the front door, just in case she had to get off the bus quickly.

"I thought you were going to Jericho Beach?" said the driver.

"Yes. Is this the place to get off the bus?"

"You mean the 'Bus Stop'?"

"Yes. 'Bus Stop'."

"No, that's a long way off.'"

"How can you tell?"

"Because I know where Jericho Beach is, "he chuckled, "It's nearly the end of my route."

"No. I mean, how can I know, every block looks the same to me," she said, a bit frustrated at not knowing the system.

"Oh, I see what you mean. OK, you see any numbers on any of the stores we're passing?"

"No. Oh, Yes! 2 – 4- 3 – 7. And now, 2 – 4 - 4 -5. Hey, they are getting larger!" she observed.

"That's right. Do you know where Main Street is?

"Yes! Actually I do. That is where the train station is at Science World, at the end of False Creek, right?"

"Yes. You know your way around this city! Well, that's 'zero'. All the streets count up from there on the west side, and count up the other way on the east side. Each block is about '100' long."

Her engineering mind quickly calculated. "So we are twenty-four blocks from Main Street! How many blocks from Main Street is Jericho Beach?"

"Oh, it's about the forty-four hundred block."

"So I have twenty more blocks to go? And all I have to do is watch for forty-four hundred on a business door?"

"That's right, in principle, but it gets even better. I'll tell you when we get there. Besides, there are no more shops by that time, just a few apartments and lots of park space, no numbers. So just relax and I'll let you know."

"Thank you!" Sumiko sat down on a seat near the front of the bus. For the first time on the bus ride she began to relax, no longer worried about missing her stop. As she watched the street scenes outside her window she automatically began to keep track of what 'hundred block' she was passing. Thirty-two hundred, thirty-three hundred. It was easy when you could see an address on a shop door. Then she noticed that at every side street there as a sign posted on a light pole, with "4th Ave" on one sign, and "Arbutus" on the other sign, at ninety degrees to the 4th Ave sign was "Blenheim Street." The signs also had the 'hundred blocks' written on them in smaller letters. Very logical, thought Sumiko.

Then she smiled and leaned close to the window when she saw something written in Japanese, 'Hitoe Sushi'. She only had a quick glimpse, but saw that it was at thirty-three forty-seven. So the address must be 3347 West 4th Avenue.

Sumiko's understanding of the city was growing at every moment. Now, she thought to herself, no matter where she is, she will be able to find things. If she is at 2900 West 3rd Ave she can walk one block farther away from the water and be on 4th Ave, then walk four and a half blocks to the west, with the mountains over her right shoulder, and find some authentic Japanese sushi!

Soon enough, the bus passed a large park by the ocean, and then a forested area, and then the bus turned down a curving road towards the beach, and pulled to a stop.

"This is your stop, young lady! Are you going to the Youth Hostel?"

"Yes. Is it far?"

"Can you see that old wooden building?"

"Yes."

"Walk past that, and the Jericho Beach Hostel is the next building, an old World War Two building, you can't miss it!"

Getting off the bus, Sumiko looked back at the driver and smiled at him, "Thank you!"

Five minutes later, she was signing in for a three night stay at the Jericho Beach Youth Hostel. It was very basic accommodations, but that was fine from Sumiko's perspective. She did not need much.

Looking around at some of the other guests in and around the lobby, she thought that most seemed friendly; however a few of them looked a bit creepy. She would have to keep a close eye on her stuff and never leave her purse or valuables unattended. Sumiko had read about how youth hostels are a great way to travel but that there are also a few creeps mixed in, just looking for a chance to rip you off.

She was already thinking defensively when a tall young man approached her. He was dressed well enough in a red Gortex wind-breaker. By the meticulous way that he appeared to keep his goatee beard trimmed, the initial impression he gave was that of someone very vain and self-absorbed. Sumiko decided right then and there, even before he opened his mouth, that he was a scumbag.

"Hello there. I see that you are new here, anything I can do to help?" he crooned.

Sumiko wanted nothing to do with him, but she wanted to be polite nonetheless.

"No thank you. I don't need any help."

"Well, my name is Frank Richards, and I'm here to help you anyhow. Let me show you around the hostel." He tried to lead her away from the reception area, touching her elbow with his hand and gently pushing her off balance.

Sumiko dug her heels in, and repeated herself more strongly. "No, thank you," and turned away from him without looking back.

The interaction with 'the goat', as Sumiko thought of the young man with the goatee really put Sumiko in a bad mood. Up until that moment, even the strange guy on the Bus, who got off at Spuzzum, had not invaded her privacy. But this goat boy, actually putting his hand on her elbow as if to lead her away under his control, had actually scared her that there were such creeps around. Who knows what he would do to a less self-confident young girl, she thought to herself.

Twenty minutes later, after settling into her dormitory and making her bed, rolling out her sleeping bag and putting the pillow case on the rather smelly pillow provided by the Hostel, she changed into warmer clothes and headed out to find the beach.

It was not difficult to find. She could see the north shore mountains so she knew that all she had to do was walk towards them and she would find that water. It had to be between her middle finger and right-ring finger.

After walking just a few hundred meters she saw the water. As she continued walking, she saw another old building left over from the Second World War. Unlike the former military barracks that the Youth Hostel now inhabited, the building in front of her seemed to serve an altogether different purpose. In preparing for her homestay in Vancouver, Sumiko had read that the entire Jericho Beach area had once been an Air Force base where a variety of sea-planes operated during the Second World War. The float planes had been there to patrol the west coast of North America for any signs of the Japanese navy, and any hot air balloons sent from Japan with bombs on them. Sumiko was surprised to learn that Japan had sent these balloons with incendiary devices, with the intent to start massive forest fires. She was also shocked to learn of how badly Japanese Canadians had been treated during the war, with their property confiscated and their liberty stripped from them, being locked up in internment camps during the war.

But Sumiko also knew that Canadian and British soldiers had been treated terribly by the Japanese as well, after being captured in Hong Kong. Thinking about the wartime history made her sad at first, as it reminded her of how much she hated war and the terrible things people do to each other in the name of their nations and their gods. But then Sumiko imagined how it could have been a nice place to fly an airplane. She thought about her hero, Amelia Earhart, and how beautiful Vancouver looked from the window of her JAL 747 when Sumiko first arrived in Vancouver. What a wonderful place to fly around, and not actually fight any battles, she thought as she explored the former military base.

Once she reached the military building along the shoreline, she saw the sign: 'Jericho Beach Sailing Centre', and decided to take a closer look.

When she passed through the wide open gate, nobody stopped her to ask her what she was doing. It was just another example of the way that you can come and go as you please in most places, without encountering any barriers.

She discovered that there was a sailing club and a windsurfing club. These were not 'members only' types of clubs, but rather, places you could just show up and sign up for a lesson or rent a board and go windsurfing. It was her kind of place. It reminded her a bit of her favorite water-craft club on Lake Biwa, in Shiga Ken. Sumiko had learned to windsurf one summer, when she had been dating Kenichi. That romance had not lasted long, about as long as Kenichi's short-lived career in Engineering school. In the end, the fact that a beach-bum and fun loving guy like Kenichi would not make it through Engineering school was no surprise. But she had no regrets. Her time with Kenichi had been a great deal of fun. She had learned to windsurf, had some passionate nights, and ultimately gotten over the break-up by refocusing her energies into her studies.

After reminiscing about her summer with Kenichi, and wandering around the Sailing Centre, Sumiko decided to come back in the summertime and do some windsurfing. She made a mental note to check out 'Windsure Windsurfing' when the season starts up again in May.

The shoreline in front of the Sailing Center had beautiful, clean, sand. The view of the city, of Stanley Park, and of the north shore mountains was simply breathtaking. Sumiko decided that the Jericho Beach area would be one of her favorite places in the city.

Walking along the shoreline, she soon discovered a long wooden pier jutting out into the waters of Burrard Inlet. At the end of the pier, she found a few Asian men throwing something into the water. Feeling safe and comfortable in 'her' city, Sumiko approached the men and struck up a conversation.

"Hello! Can you please tell me, what are you doing?"

The older of the two men smiled a toothy grin. He seemed so nice and even if his face was dirty, missing a few teeth, and a complete stranger, Sumiko was not at all afraid to talk to him.

"Crab. We get crab. Sometimes lotta crab. Today no crab. Diver took crab."

Sumiko realized that his English was not very good, but understood that they were fishing for crab.

"Thank you. Can I watch?"

"Yes. Maybe you throw trap? Want throw?"

"Yes, please!" Sumiko was delighted.

With the old man's help, she held the coiled up fishing rope in one hand and hefted the triangular fish trap with the other. It was heavy. There was a fish's head tied to the middle, and it was clear to the Engineer in Sumiko that the trap was designed to splay open when it sunk to the bottom. Then, when you pull it back up out of the water, any crabs that had been feasting on the fish head would suddenly be trapped as the triangles of the four-sided trap closed.

She threw the net out. It made a big splash and then sunk below the surface.

Just then, a scuba diver surfaced not far way. So that was what the old man meant. Divers are also collecting crabs. That seemed so unfair! They could simply swim around and grab the crabs, and the poor old fisherman had little chance to compete.

She watched as the diver swam to a nearby floating dock and his wife passed a large plastic bucket into the water. The diver put the crabs into the bucket and pushed it up, helping his wife pull the heavy bucket back up and place it on the dock.

Sumiko walked over to the stairs that lead down to the dock, to take a look. After walking down the steep staircase, from the pier to the floating dock down on the surface of the water, she walked close enough to the lady and the diver, and peeked into the bucket.

The bucket was full of crabs. But the next thing the diver did surprised Sumiko. He took the crabs out, one at a time, and measured them against a wooden stick with markings on it. After checking their size, the diver threw each crab back into the ocean!

"Excuse me! Why are you throwing them away?" Sumiko asked.

"They're too small. They have to be six inches or longer."

"Oh. So you throw them back so they can grow larger?"

"That's right. We usually only keep two or three." When he was done, there were only three crabs left in the bucket, larger than the ones he had thrown away.

Satisfied that she had learned something interesting, Sumiko went back up to the Asian men.

They were just starting to reel in the ropes, pulling their traps out of the water. Sumiko recognized 'her' trap, and was excited to see that it was full of crabs! Their pincers and legs were moving about wildly, and they tried to run in all directions when the men opened one side of the crab trap. They threw all five crabs into their own plastic bucket and then threw the trap back into the water, the fish-head having been partly eaten by the crabs.

Sumiko was surprised that the men did not measure the crabs. They seemed to be keeping all of the crabs.

She decided not to ask. These men were obviously much poorer than the diver, so they probably did not care about conservation, she reasoned.

After hanging around on the pier for another half-hour, Sumiko wandered farther along the beach, up into the wind, to the west.

When she passed some sort of outdoor restaurant, obviously closed for the season, she realized that it was just one of many. As far as the eye could see, along the beach to the west, there was another one of these beach concession stands every half-kilometer or so. The name on the closest one was 'Spanish Banks'. That must be the name of this stretch of beach, she thought.

Feeling suddenly very cold and hungry, Sumiko turned around and began to walk back towards the youth hostel. Rather than walking along the beach, however, she decided to follow a path through a forest park. It was beautiful. Most of the trees were dark green, with those heavy hanging arms of evergreen that she knew were cedars. But her enjoyment was cut short.

The path she was on took her towards a man sitting by a log eating an orange. She recognized the man, even from behind. It was the goat boy.

She did not want to interact with goat boy, so she turned 180 degrees and walked back up the beach. Perhaps there was a bit of anger in her now, at almost having had to look at the creep again, but Sumiko was no longer tired or hungry. She suddenly had her second wind.

So she walked past the Spanish Banks concession, and walked another two kilometers up the beach.

She got all the way to a point where the long beach and park disappeared into rising terrain. Sitting on a log, looking out towards Georgia Strait, Sumiko opened her day-pack and took out her map of Vancouver. She saw that just around the corner from where she was, there was a nudist beach called 'Wreck Beach'.

It made her blush to think about going nude on a public beach. There was no way on earth that Sumiko would do that, she thought. Then, with a mischievous smile to herself, she imagined that under the right circumstances, maybe she could go topless.

She took an apple form her day-pack and sat there for a while, watching a cruise ship moving across the water on the distant horizon. What an incredible place, she thought.

On her walk back to the youth hostel, Sumiko suddenly realized that she was at the log where Goat boy had been sitting. He had left a mess of orange peels and a pop bottle.

"What a pig!" she blurted out loud. Unable to leave such a disgraceful mess in such a beautiful place, Sumiko took a plastic bag out of a 'doggie doodie' plastic bag dispenser, where dog-walkers could take plastic bags to collect dog poop, and gathered up all the peels and the pop bottle.

Ten minutes later, when she returned to the youth hostel, she saw Goat Boy hassling another young girl in the common area of the hostel. Just like Sumiko, this young girl wanted nothing to do with the jerk, and walked away from him as if he were contagious.

The girl looked back at Goat Boy just as Sumiko walked up to him.

"Hey! You forgot your garbage on the beach!" Sumiko said, handing the doggie-do bag to the litter-bug so abruptly that he instinctively accepted it without realizing what it was. Sumiko was completely surprised by what she had just done. It had been unplanned. She had planned to find a garbage bin and just throw the litter away, but what she had done, impromptu as it was, had been perfect.

"That's not my garbage, take it back!" he said.

"It is your garbage. I saw you leave it. So you lie!" Sumiko said, and then she turned and walked away. She was momentarily afraid that he would do something about it, bother her in some way, but then suddenly the young girl and several other people in the common area erupted in cheers!

Sumiko smiled, and continued walking through the common area, towards the exit to her dormitory, feeling like a champion. The smiles and friendly looks from the other people in the youth hostel, and the way that Goat Boy quietly left the building in embarrassment, made Sumiko feel as if she had just reclaimed the youth hostel from the unpleasant young man, as if she had liberated the space for everybody.

13

ARRIVAL DO-OVER

Sumiko had spent the last week staying with Doris in her condo near Athlete's Village. She had enjoyed their long walks with Bella to Granville Island and Sumiko had reactivated some of Doris's long lost Japanese language skills.

On her thirtieth day in Canada, Sumiko repacked her packsack and headed out to finally begin her homestay. Only this time her journey was much shorter. After a five minute walk to the Olympic Village Skytrain station and a two minute wait for the Skytrain bound for Vancouver International Airport, YVR, Sumiko was just 22 minutes from "arriving" in Vancouver.

She had not decided how she would handle the moment when she would meet up with her homestay family and it had bothered her a great deal. She had tossed and turned for the last few nights, particularly when she had called her homestay family and had not found a way to tell them that she was already in Vancouver. She knew that she had lied, even if only by omission.

She felt like a character in a love story. She was keeping a terrible secret that would destroy the relationship when it would ultimately come to the surface, and she hadn't even met her homestay family yet.

The only thing to do was to step into it and do her best to make it turn out well. She knew in her heart that honesty was the only way. She also knew that timing was everything.

Sean and Jennifer Goodwin along with their daughter, Katie, and son, Andrew, had arrived early at the airport. Sumiko's entire homestay family was standing by the short brick wall that separated the arrivals area from the public reception area. They had been watching passengers come through the door that led from the Customs and Immigration area.

They had a sign written very well in Japanese, saying "Welcome to Canada, Sumiko Kichida!" Young Katie had been working on her Japanese calligraphy, shodo, to get the sign just right.

Sumiko saw it after sneaking into the flow of passengers with her packsack on her back as though she had just cleared through Canada Customs. She immediately recognized her homestay family from the photographs she had seen online.

From the slightly off-sloped lettering and wobbly brush strokes Sumiko surmised that the sign had been done by a well-intended child, her homestay sister. She felt a wave of love in her heart for Katie and a pang of homesickness for her own little sister, Aiko.

Trying to sound like she had just gotten of the plane from Japan, with the typical pronunciation errors she used to make all the time, Sumiko approached the Goodwins.

"Herro. Me Sumiko. Homestay family you?"

"Yes, Sumiko, were are the Goodwins. I'm Jennifer, This is my husband, Sean, our son, Andrew, and our daughter, Katie. We are so happy to finally meet you," said Jennifer, as she reached out to embrace Sumiko.

Sumiko caught herself opening up and leaning into the embrace, just as she had embraced Doris a few hours earlier. Then she caught herself and shied away in a more typically Japanese manner.

After an awkward silence, Andrew got things moving again. "Can I take your packsack, Sumiko?"

"Hai, arigato, dozo," said Sumiko, playing the shy little Japanese girl, trying to appear bewildered as she looked around the arrivals lounge as though for the first time.

As she was doing this she felt like she was digging herself a deeper and deeper hole. But she also intuited that it was not the right time to try to explain what had happened to her over the past month. She had made her bed, and now had to lie in it for a while, so to speak.

The Goodwins asked her all about her flight from Osaka. Sumiko tried to remember a few of the highlights of her actual flight, a month prior, and retold the story of being upgraded to First Class. Andrew thought that was 'very cool'.

It was not difficult for Sumiko to appear excited during the drive from the airport towards downtown Vancouver, as she stared wide-eyed out, taking in everything she could see through the window of the Goodwins' Suburban. Even after over a week exploring the west side of Vancouver on her own, Sumiko had still not had a ride in a car in Canada, let alone a massive SUV like the Goodwins's suburban. Sitting so much higher than the other cars, riding in the SUV was a lot of fun for Sumiko. It allowed her to see over the other cars and look at the houses and storefronts as they drove up Granville from the Arthur Lang Bridge into Oakridge and then down Granville towards 9th Avenue.

Sumiko knew that she was crossing over the middle finger of the city and would soon be on Granville Bridge over False Creek and then on into downtown. She tried to look over the side of the bridge to see False Creek but the bridge was so wide that she could not see much of anything. She could see the silvery geodesic dome of Science World farther away to the east, at the head of False Creek.

All the way along, Katie was asking her question after question while Andrew was doing his best imitation of a tour guide, calling out the names of neighborhoods, streets and buildings as they passed by. Sumiko knew some of them already but most of them were new. She felt as though she were arriving in a new city after all.

When the Goodwins turned West and drove along Alberni Street, Sumiko made a mental note of the location of 'Kobe Japanese Steak House' in the first block of Alberni Street after turning off from Burrard Street.

Soon enough they were entering Stanley Park. Sumiko had 'saved' Stanley Park and had not visited it yet so that she could experience it for the first time with her homestay family. Just days prior, Jennifer Goodwin had emailed her their plan to show her around Vancouver. Replying 'from Japan', Sumiko had told them how excited she was that they were going to show her around, to make her know her way around the city until she knew it 'like the back of her hand', as Sean had put it. That really made Sumiko smile, as she had been using the back of her hand to navigate around the city ever since she had originally arrived. But having Stanley Park, Grouse Mountain, Lonsdale Quay and so many other Vancouver highlights in the Goodwin's plan for her made Sumiko's arrival do-over feel like her true arrival in Vancouver.

What Sumiko did not know was what Jennifer was thinking. Jennifer was an experienced ESL teacher and had noticed that there was something wrong with the way Sumiko was speaking English. For someone just off the JAL flight from Japan, thought Jennifer, Sumiko had an excellent ear for English. She had seemed to understand almost all of the constant barrage she was receiving from Andrew and Katie, and she had not once asked what something meant or for a repetition of a difficult word. Also, Sumiko seemed to be inconsistent in the errors she was making when she spoke. At times, Sumiko was using 'B's where there should be 'V's', and 'R' when it should be an "L". But at other times, flawless pronunciation slipped out.

Sumiko was noticing it too. The deception was difficult to keep up. It started to make Sumiko feel terrible so she began to talk less and less, pretending to be tired from her flight.

Sensing this, Jennifer threw her a lifeline. "Andrew, Katie, let's let Sumiko have some peace and quiet. I'm sure she's exhausted after such a long flight and all the new information you've given her."

"Thank you. Yes, I tiringed, but I also very happy to here," said Sumiko.

They passed through the Stanley Park Causeway and over Lions Gate Bridge in silence. Even so, Sumiko literally gasped at the beauty of the bridge crossing, and let out an "ooh!" when she saw an enormous cruise ship passing under the bridge as they crossed over it. Her Japanese character took hold and she pulled out her digital camera and snapped some pictures like the excited Japanese tourist that she was.

"Sumiko, can you see that mountain with the line cut up through the trees?" asked Andrew.

"Yes. It is beautiful. What is her name?"

"That's Grouse Mountain. We live near the bottom of it in Edgemont Village."

"Edgemontont Billage?" Sumiko asked, holding back a laugh.

"No, that sounds like Edmonton! No, it's Edge-Mont Village."

"Edge-Mont Billage," Sumiko tried to say imperfectly, and then added "Vancouver is so very beautiful. I just love it!"

Sean and Jennifer exchanged a serious, knowing look. Sumiko noticed it, and understood. She had just pronounced a series of 'Vs' and 'L's perfectly and naturally. She was proud of her improved English pronunciation while also ashamed at the lie she had been maintaining.

After an uncomfortable pause, Andrew continued his tour guide narrative.

"This is Marine Drive. If you go that way, you end up in West Vancouver, where the rich people live. If you go this way," just as the car turned to the right, onto Northwest Marine Drive, "you enter

North Vancouver. We turn here, and head towards Grouse Mountain."

A few minutes later, Sean pulled the Suburban into the family driveway and turned off the car.

"We're here! Home sweet home! Welcome to the Goodwin home!"

As the family got out of the Suburban, Sumiko glanced at the well-manicured lawn in front of the house. There was a beautiful swing-seat made out of large cedar branches and logs. With the sun shining and the lush green of the lawn, it made a peaceful sight.

Sumiko needed peace. She needed to clear her conscience. She could not let the lie continue one minute longer.

"Mrs. Jennifer? Could we please sit together on that bench? I have something I must to discuss with you right now," Sumiko said.

A very intuitive woman, Jennifer understood that Sumiko needed to talk, woman to woman. "Of course, Sumiko, let's go. "Guys, take Sumiko's bags in and wait for us inside, we'll be a few minutes – girl talk!"

From inside the house, Sean looked out the kitchen window to see how they were doing. Sumiko was doing all the talking, and Jennifer was nodding her head.

Ten minutes later, when Sean looked out again Sumiko was talking just as fast but she looked more relaxed, even smiling at times. He could see that Jennifer was smiling as well, throwing her head back in laughter at times with her hand gently placed on Sumiko's shoulder. Sean knew what that meant. It meant that everything was OK between the two women, whatever the problem had been. He figured it had something to do with Sumiko's actual level of English and the way she had seemed to be faking some of her pronunciation errors.

After confessing to Jennifer, Sumiko felt a thousand times better. She had retold the story of the last month, from her month-too-early arrival at YVR to her unplanned VIA Rail trip to Edmonton, her side trip to Yellowknife and even the handsome man whose blue eyes still haunted her soul.

Sumiko and Jennifer understood each other and became fast friends. Jennifer was impressed with

Sumiko's command of English but even more so with Sumiko's good character.

Jennifer led Sumiko into the house, truly happy to be welcoming such a nice girl into the family.

14

MAKE YOURSELF AT HOME

Sumiko's first impression of the Goodwin home, from the outside, was that it was a simple box. Despite the beautiful and lush landscaping of the very large front yard, the house itself seemed to have no style at all. It was just a two-level box to house people in. She looked at the other houses along the street. They also looked like boxes. And on the roof, she could see, some kind of moss was growing on the roof tiles. She liked that. It made it seem like the rainforest was trying to attack the houses and replace them with natural life.

If the outside of the house was a disappointment, the inside made up for it. It was beautiful. There was a beautiful tile floor at the entrance and hardwood floors in the other rooms on the main floor.

Sumiko noticed that the family had all taken their shoes off at the entrance, similar to Japanese people, however they just walked around the house in their socks. Only Mrs. Goodwin put on a pair of slippers. There was a pair of cheap slippers left out for Sumiko.

"These are for you, Sumiko. We don't wear homeshoes much here in Canada. Most people just walk around in socks in our family. You can do whatever you like," explained Jennifer.

As nice as the entrance to the house seemed to Sumiko, it seemed very strange and foreign to her. It did not have the close intimacy of her home in Kyoto. Everything just seemed to be too large. For the first time in her trip she wondered if maybe she had made a mistake in choosing the Goodwin family but she tried to be polite and give it a chance anyhow. She reminded herself that she was not here to live in the Japanese style but to learn about how Canadian lived and not to pass judgment.

"Thank you. These will be fine, but I have my own homeshoes in my pack."

"I thought you would bring your own, but you'll need them for downstairs."

"Downstairs?"

"You'll understand in a minute, but first, Andrew, why don't you give Sumiko the twenty-five cent tour?"

"Sure, Mom. Sue! That's what I'm going to call you, OK, Sumiko? Come with me!"

"Yes, OK, call me Sue. I am coming, And. Can I call you And?

"And? Well, actually, 'Andy' is better."

"Thanks, Andy. By the way, what does 'twenty-five cent tour' mean?"

"You get what you paid for. How much of a tour do you think you could get for a quarter?"

"A quarter, yes, twenty-five cents. Not much?"

"You got it, Pontiac. You are very quick on the uptake, Sue."

Andrew showed Sumiko all around the house, giving her far more than twenty-five cents worth. Sumiko was very impressed with how big the house was and the way that every person had their own room. But she found the house to be much more cluttered than a Japanese home would be.

When she saw Andrew's room, she was amazed. His walls were literally covered with posters of all sorts. Pictures of snowboarding, skiing, windsurfing and other sports, along with a few racy pictures of bikini-clad women.

"Do you do all of these sports, Andy?"

"Yup. But mostly snowboarding."

"Aaaah. I understand. You must to do snowboarding in Goose Mountain?"

Andrew made a face at that, trying to understand what she meant, and then smiled. "No, I actually don't like going up Grouse all that much – too many bowling pins and dragons up there, and lots of arctic cougars as well. No, my buds and I go up to Whistler to do our airdogging and cutting the pow pow. You should have seen the conditions up there last week, it was epic! But you'll see soon enough. I got Mom to cut you loose for a day of snowboarding with me this Saturday. I'll teach you how. Or have you ever tried It In Japan?"

"Actually, I am a hotdog," replied Sumiko, surprising Andrew that she knew what he was talking about in snowboarder slang.

"You're not a poser, I hope! But we'll see soon enough."

"Andrew! Sumiko! Come on downstairs!" called Sean, ending the house tour.

Sumiko was a bit surprised to see that in Canada people just yell out loudly. It was yet another contrast to how people live in Japan, where such shouting would be considered to be impolite.

When Sumiko and Andrew joined the rest of the family at the kitchen table, Sumiko was starting to feel a bit more comfortable but she still had not been shown where she would sleep. Perhaps they would roll out a futon for her in one of the children's rooms, she thought. But what she really hoped was that there would be a room just for her, where she could have some privacy.

"Sumiko, you must be tired after all that travel. Would you like to see your 'a pat o'?"

"A pat o? What is that, Mr. Sean."

"Just call me Sean. Your apartment."

"Apartment? I thought I was going to live here with your family?" Sumiko was excited and alarmed. She wanted to spend a lot of time with the family, to improve her English, but the idea of having her own apartment sounded great.

Suddenly in imperfect but understandable Japanese, Sean explained that Sumiko has her own four-tsubo apartment. She could come and go through her own entry but she must not have guests over after midnight. At least not without permission.

"You speak Japanese! Your Japanese is so good, Mr. Sean. Why do you speak Japanese?"

"I lived in Tokyo for two years, but that's a long story," he replied, in English. "Anyhow, I hope you'll have a little time to help me with my Japanese. It's so hard to retain my language skills. Not all of our homestay guests are Japanese, you see."

"Yes, I would love to help you! But your Japanese is very good," she replied in Japanese.

"Thanks. Anyhow, here's the key to your 'apaato'. I think you'll find everything you need there. And just to make it more fun for you I would like you to go there all by yourself and don't come back until 6pm, dinner time!" he said with a mischievous smile.

"By myself? OK, that would be nice. Where do I go?" asked Sumiko, accepting the key from Sean.

Holding the back door open for Sumiko, he said: "Just head out into the back yard, take a look around, and then try your key out in that big door at the bottom of the stairs. You'll figure it out. Think of it as a treasure hunt!"

"I like treasure hunts!" replied Sumiko as she hefted her packsack back onto her shoulder and went out onto the back deck.

The deck itself had a nice set of patio furniture, a large appliance that Sumiko thought could be a barbeque, and at the far end, surrounded by some type of cedar lattice work, Sumiko saw a hot tub.

After descending the wooden staircase from the deck, Sumko explored the back yard. There was a large expanse of green lawn making a square about twenty metres across, and what looked like an apple tree towards the back. All around the yard there was a cedar fence with a strip of lattice work along the top. There were also several tall cedar trees making a wall of green hedges on the opposite sides of the fence, perhaps in the neighbor's yard. It made for a quiet, natural space that somehow made Sumiko feel happy. She liked cedar trees. They reminded her of some of her favorite forest parks in Japan.

After looking around the yard she turned back to the house and tried her key in the door at the bottom of the stairs.

The key slid in smoothly. She turned it, feeling the solid hardware as the key rotated in the tumbler.

Sumiko felt a great deal of excitement as she pushed the door open. Somehow it felt like a momentous occasion, as though her intuition was telling here that this place would be important to her, that something good was going to happen to her here.

When she entered, she was not disappointed.

After crossing the threshold and pulling the door closed behind her she was immediately transported 7,500 kilometers to the west, to Japan.

The entrance to the basement suite in the Goodwin home had been renovated to resemble a Japanese home. There was a genkan, a Japanese entrance foyer, where she found several pairs of slippers, presumably for herself and any guests she might have. There were two steps up from the genkan into the rest of the suite and hardwood flooring throughout. There was even a tall brass cylinder with three or four umbrellas standing inside. It was actually very similar to the entrance to the Kichida family home.

Stepping out of her sneakers and slipping on a pair of slippers Sumiko placed her shoes on the wooden shelf just to the one side and then entered her apartment, her apaato, already feeling at home.

It took her a few minutes to find the light switch, in the dim light coming through the heavily curtained windows. Once she found a light switch in the hallway and turned on some lights she could see everything much more clearly.

To her right there as a large room with a couch, a table, an armchair and a big screen television. Her very own living room! At the other end of this large open space there was a kitchen and a small table with four chairs. She would be able to prepare her own food and even have her own late-night snacks without bothering the family upstairs. Very nice.

Then Sumiko looked through the open doorway to her left. Tatami mats! A futon! Her bedroom was appointed in traditional Japanese style, she realized. It must be something that Mr. Sean brought back from Japan, she thought, or at least had found a way to duplicate here in Canada. And that was not the end of it. There were even more surprises in store for her in the bathroom.

Unlike the long, shallow bathtubs that she had found in the hotel rooms she had stayed at so far in Canada, the bathroom in her apartment had a furo! A genuine Japanese bathtub. It was a simple steel box, about 90 cm by 90cm by 90 cm, just the perfect size for a person to sit cross-legged in with hot water up to one's neck and have a great long hot bath! And there was a tiled floor with a drain in front of the furo, with a small wooden stool, a bucket, and some coral sponge. Next to this there was a shower wand with hot and cold water taps. On the floor, there was a red plastic bucket with a bar of soap in a plastic tray and a clean facecloth folded neatly on top. Everything she needed to have a proper wash before going into the furo.

Without missing a beat, Sumiko found the plug for the furo and opened the taps. Soon piping hot water began to fill the furo.

Stripping down to her underwear Sumiko paused for a moment. She looked around to make sure that the doors were closed and that she would have privacy. After latching the door just to make sure, she finally relaxed and took the rest of her clothes off and got down to the business of giving herself a thoroughly Japanese scrub, sitting on the wooden stool. After 15 minutes of washing and rinsing, she was ready for her bath.

Sumiko must have spent thirty minutes just soaking in the furo, letting the heat penetrate through her body.

Absolutely relaxed and in a peaceful, meditative state, Sumiko found her thoughts wandering, half asleep. She was not even sure what she was thinking about, only that she felt calm and at peace.

It was not until she rolled out the futon, set her mechanical alarm clock and settled into bed under the quilt that she found tucked away in a closet in her bedroom that Sumiko realized why she felt so good.

She was home.

And her new home made her feel more at home than she had felt in years, perhaps even her entire life. Something, she mused, something important is going to happen to me in this place.

Five hours later, Sumiko woke up from her completely unnecessary nap and joined her homestay family for dinner.

The dinner was decidedly not Japanese. It was Sean Goodwin's signature meal, spaghetti casserole.

As Sumiko tentatively ate the unfamiliar meal, she listened to Sean and Jennifer explain the family routine and the rules of the house.

They gave her a binder that they had built up over several years of hosting ESL homestay students. The binder contained all sorts of resources that Sumiko could make use of. There was a bus route map of the greater Vancouver area, travel pamphlets, and all sorts of pamphlets about local sightseeing activities.

Later, back in her apartment getting ready for her first night at home, Sumiko explored the small bookshelf. It had all sorts of tourist activity books, a variety of foreign language-to-English dictionaries, and photography books about Vancouver and about Canada.

15

SEA TO SKY

Andy drove like an old woman, Sumiko thought to herself. With so much room and so few cars, she wondered why he was being so careful not to speed. In Japan the only time there would be this much open space on the highway would be late at night, a great time for young people to open up and see what their cars could do.

"You are a very carefully driver, Andy."

"Thanks, Sue, my Dad had me take Driver's ed last year. I got my license right away when I turned 16, and now I've been driving with passengers for about six months. But it all goes away if I get even one single ticket, dad says."

"You will lose your license?"

"Not exactly. It gets complicated. If I get a ticket, then the cost to insure my car goes up, when I eventually buy my own car. But no. Dad says that if I get a ticket or anything like an avoidable accident then he will not let me drive any of the family cars, and not even anybody else's car, for at least a year. I don't want that to happen, so I have to drive defensively – take no chances."

"That explains why you are staying at the speed limit when all these other cars are going faster," Sumiko observed.

"Yeah. It bugged me at first, but you know what? All these cars that blow past me will be caught up in traffic jams along the way. They won't get there any faster than we will. In fact, we'll probably pass a few. Like those guys right there!" Andrew pointed at a car pulled over at the side of the road with a police car parked behind, red and blue lights flashing. Obviously pulled over for a speeding ticket.

"See you on the slopes, suckers!" Andrew said as they passed the unfortunate speeders. Sumiko caught a glimpse of the police officer handing a paper ticket to the driver.

"Why do they have a man on a horse painted on the police car door?"

"Because those are 'pony soldiers', RCMP."

"RCMP? Oh, 'Royal Canadian Mounted Police', right?"

"That's right, Sue. They used to ride on horses, and still do for parades and sometimes for crowd control, like at hockey riots."

"What is hockey riot?"

"A hockey riot is when our hockey team, the Vancouver Canucks, gets eliminated from the Stanley Cup finals in game seven. The city erupts into chaos and the police have to arrest hundreds of window-smashing hooligans," Andrew explained.

"People really take their hockey seriously here", observed Sumiko. Then she remembered something funny her English teacher in Japan had said, and decided to try to retell the story to Andrew and his friends.

"When I was studying English in Japan, my teacher, David, explained the rules about hockey and then we went to an ice hockey game. He had told us all about icing cake the puck,"

"You mean 'icing'," interrupted one of the guys in the back seat.

"Thanks. Yes, icing the puck, off-side, short-handed goals, power-play, and my favorite rule, empty-net goal!" Sumiko continued. "But he also told us a rule that we did not understand at first. He said that there is a special rule for the play-offs." Sumiko said, with a smile, hoping one of the boys would take the bait.

"What is that?"

"The rule that says that when a team is eliminated from the play-offs they have to go and play golf and hang their heads in great shame - because they were eliminated! David said that it is not money or their career goals, but that this shame is the real motivation for winning and advancing in the play-offs, to keep playing hockey as long as possible into the spring and summer and never have to play golf!"

All three boys broke out in laughter.

The drive up the Sea-to-Sky highway had been beautiful. Sumiko felt that she was fitting in with the Andrew and his two friends, as they drove together in the Goodwin family's spare car, an old Volkswagon Gulf.

Sumiko could not get enough of the beautiful scenery along the way from North Vancouver to the tip of her baby finger, at Horseshoe Bay.

As they passed the BC Ferries Terminal at Horseshoe Bay, Sumiko looked down the cliff and saw a large ferry boat just pulling into the dock.

She knew that the Goodwin family had put a day-trip to visit Sechelt, on the Sunshine Coast, into the itinerary for Sumiko's first few weeks as a homestay guest. So she would soon have an opportunity to see the ferry boat up close. For now, she kept her focus on the day-trip with Andrew, to go snow-boarding up at Whistler and Blackcomb mountains.

Looking out her window to the right, Sumiko noticed that there was an older highway hidden in the forest, beside the newly improved Sea-to-Sky highway. Judging by the many curves and dips of the old highway, compared with the smooth curves of the new road, Sumiko figured that driving up the old highway would have been much more difficult. It reminded her of the highway from Kyoto to Lake Biwa, in Shiga Ken. When her parents drove them out there to visit their cousins, little Aiko would become car sick. But on this beautiful new highway, the long drive along the edge of the mountains with the waters of Howe Sound below on the left and the snow-frosted mountains all around, Sumiko was comfortable and relaxed as she took in all of the scenery.

Hours later she was sitting with the boys as they rode up Excalibur gondola for yet another run. Sumiko was having a wonderful sunny day of snowboarding at Whistler – Blackcomb. As much as the snowboarding was fun, she was no-where near as advanced as the three young men from North Vancouver.

As the day wore on Sumiko realized that she may have bitten off more than she could chew and that she was getting very tired. She knew that doing extreme sports like snowboarding could be dangerous, especially when one gets tired. So she spoke up.

"Guys, I am getting very tiring. I need to take a break. Do you mind if I go back to the Village and look around? You guys keep going."

"No way, Sue. First of all, you are never 'tiring', but you may be getting 'tired'. Second, we're showing you around today. We come up here all the time and this is your first time here, so if you're getting tired then it's time for an early supper! Let's boogie down to the Village!"

Without waiting for her answer all three boys set off down the hill, carving gnarly tracks all the way to the bottom.

Sumiko took her time, falling farther behind all the way. It was to be her last run of the day and she wanted to enjoy every second of it. She loved the way her breath turned to white cloud as she exhaled. She enjoyed the fresh feeling as the cold air rushed into her lungs. The frost on the trees reminded her of Christmas decorations and the view from the mountain top to the valley below was simply breathtaking.

Forty five minutes later they had all put their boards and snowboarding gear away in the VW Golf and were walking around in Whistler Village. The boys really knew their way around. They told Sumiko which were the best bars and restaurants. Eventually they arrived at their favorite haunt, the Brewhouse.

The atmosphere in the Brewhouse was fabulous. There were so many attractive, well-dressed young people having fun.

"What will you have?" said the cheerful young waitress. Sumiko noticed that she had an Australian accent.

The boys ordered chicken wings, nachos seafood Caesar salads, and a Mexican kind of beer 'Dos-Ekkis', two X's. All except for Andrew, that is. He just asked for a carafe of water because he was driving and also because at 17 years old he was underage. The other boys were legal drinking age, nineteen years old.

"And for you, Miss?"

"I want to have a pizza and a beer."

"What kind of pizza?"

"Thin curst. Whole Wheat. Salami, Pepperoni, tomatoes and mushrooms. Oh, and add extra cheese, please!" said Sumiko.

"And the beer?"

"Do you have 'brewed fresh in the Kootenays?'"

"Kokanee Beer? Yes, we have that. Are you a Kokanee Rangerette or something?"

Sumiko didn't understand the last question at first but then realized that it had something to do with the beer advertising she had seen on TV while she was in Nelson. Something about pretty young girls competing for a chance to work with a forest ranger whose job was to protect the Kokanee Beer from being stolen by a big hairy monster, the Sasquatch.

"Yes, I am a Ranger! Kokanee Beer please!" Sumiko grinned, happy that she understood the reference.

Soon a man came with a long wooden paddle to stuff the pizza into the oven. He had a small cart with four uncooked pizzas laid out on it. Sumiko was very interested in how the brick pizza oven worked. There was a small fire inside, at the back of the oven, and a flat area of bricks on which the man slid the pizzas on, to bake them.

The pizza chef was an old man with a straw hat, and a nametag: 'Cornelius'. He seemed very friendly and kind, like Mr. Yamada back in Kyoto.

"Is this your pizza, my dear?" He asked Sumiko, after noticing how intently she was watching him.

"Yes, it is, Mr. Cornelius."

"Just 'Cornelius'. Would you like to bake it yourself?"

"Would I? Yes, of course, please!"

"Ok, just watch me do these three first, then I'll talk you through doing your own," he said, as he scooped the first one, a Hawaiian, onto the paddle and smoothly slid it into the back left corner. He then slid a three-cheese into the right corner and a vegetarian into the middle, towards the front of the oven.

"The flames from the wood fire cook the top of the pizza and the heat in the bricks cooks the bottom," he said.

"Aaaaah"

"You know, I can bake a chicken in this oven even two days after I let the fire out? It really holds the heat. We keep the temperature at seven hundred degrees for pizza, far more than you need to cook meat."

"Really?"

"Now watch this. You have to get the paddle under just one side and partly lift the pizza, and pull back a bit on the paddle. You see how it makes the pizza rotate? That way we don't keep it in one spot for too long and it bakes evenly. Now we turn it again, two more times, like this, and now it's time to take it out," he said, as he scooped out the three pizzas, one at a time.

"Easy. Now you try."

Sumiko felt a bit awkward at first, but soon relaxed and had fun baking her own pizza, with just a little help from old Cornelius.

By the time they finished their meal, the two 19 year olds had drank five beers, and Sumiko had drank three. Andrew, the designated driver, had only drank water.

On their way to the parking lot before driving home the boys began shoving each other around in good fun but then Andrew stumbled on a loose brick and twisted his ankle and fell to the ground.

They all found it funny at first but then Andrew really began to feel the pain. "Oooh, it really hurts! There's no way I can drive home with this. Kevin, can you drive?"

"Sure."

"Um, are you sure that is such a good idea?" asked Sumiko.

"I see what you mean, Sue. We've all had a fair amount to drink, haven't we? And we all know about Mr. Goodwin's rules for Andrew and driving, so there's no way we should risk a DUI."

"DUI?" asked Sumiko.

"Driving Under the Influence of alcohol. Usually a twenty-four hour suspension, a big ticket, and possibly much harsher consequences," explained Andrew.

"So what are we going to do," asked Kevin.

"Actually, I have a great idea," said Sumiko.

Three hours later, after checking into a very nice hotel in Whistler Village and calling their parents to tell them they had to stay the night in Whistler, the four young people were in a karaoke bar. They were all drinking beer and egging Sumiko on for yet another of her best attempts to sing songs in English. Sumiko had already promised not to tell Sean about the beers Andrew was drinking.

Sumiko reasoned that she was the oldest person there and so was really her decision to let Andrew behave as he would if she were not with him. He was a responsible young man and a few beers would do no harm, as long as they did not drink and drive.

The only thing that did not go well on that outing was how Sumiko responded to Andrew's friend, Kevin, later that night. He had tried to kiss her. She had pushed him away and made a face at him that seemed to really hurt his feelings.

It had been an innocent pass which Sumiko would normally have been complimented to receive, but for some reason Sumiko felt strongly that she could not get romantically involved with any man, even as good looking and fun as Kevin was.

Her heart belonged to another man, even if she would never see him again. It was at that moment that Sumiko realized what unrequited love really meant. It meant a lifetime of misery, unable to embrace the love of any other man, unable to find the man she had lost in Yellowknife.

16

GROUSE GRIND

She would never forget her 25th birthday. It started well, when she opened the letter from her family. She had received the letter fully three weeks before her birthday and then saved it until her actual birthday, June 5th.

The letter from her parents was routine, enough to reassure her that nothing had changed back home. The letter from Aikochan, written very carefully in English, had been heartbreaking. It made Sumiko miss her darling little sister. She could tell that Aiko missed her too. But more than that, she felt so much pride in her little sister. She really wanted to be with her to tell her so.

Rather than to hang around with the many social contacts Sumiko had made in Vancouver, or to let the Goodwin's know about her birthday, Sumiko decided to spend most of the day on her own.

It was time for her to take on a challenge, the Grouse Grind. And after waiting for the right weather conditions, she finally had good weather. To make things even better, today was Thursday, 'Mokuyoubi', 'wood day' in Japanese. As Sumiko wanted to commune with nature on the mountain, to connect with the cedar and fir trees in the forest, she thought it was fitting that she challenge herself with the Grouse Grind on wood day.

After going upstairs in the Goodwin family kitchen for a cup of coffee, Sumiko wrote a note to Jennifer, as she did each time she went out. There was an unwritten rule that Sumiko could come and go as she pleased as long as she kept Jennifer informed about where she was going, when she would be back, and how to get in contact with Sumiko if necessary.

"Dear Jennifer, I am going up the Grouse Grind and will be home by six pm. I am having dinner downstairs with some Japanese girl-friends. Please tell the family that they can join us for some shabu-shabu. We'll have enough for everybody. Love, Sumiko."

Sumiko had made close friends with two Japanese girls she had met at her part-time job. She did not really need the money, but working at the printing section of the Kinko's Copy Centre on West Broadway Street gave her lots of opportunities to interact with people in English. It was a long way to commute to from Edgemont Village in North Van, but Sumiko loved to travel across the city. She often walked down to Kitsilano Beach or along 4th Avenue after work, exploring shops and enjoying the walks. Vancouver was such a walkable city with so many unexpected little things to see and do.

The day before, she and her Japanese girlfriends had been to Chinatown to shop. They found the carefully prepared, thin cut and frozen slices of pork and top sirloin prepared especially for the Japanese shabu-shabu style of cooking. One of the girls was going to bring two propane-powered stoves. One to boil the meats on and the other for the tofu, cabbage, enokitake & shiitake mushrooms and other vegetables. Finding the soy and goma sauces was also very easy in Chinatown.

Sumiko looked forward to teaching the Goodwins all about the 'swish swish' style of cooking shabu-shabu. She was certain that the entire homestay family would take her up on her invitation.

Five minutes later she was headed out the door. She was wearing layered clothing so that she could be warm on her walk to the base of the mountain, just four kilometers up the road, and then remove one or two layers as she heated due to the strenuous effort involved in hiking up the mountain.

She was wearing a well worn-in pair of hiking boots and she had a small first-aid kit, her digital camera and a few bottles of water in a small backpack.

The walk from the Goodwin's to the foot of Grouse Mountain was more of an effort than Sumiko had expected. The road was up-hill all the way so she had to pace herself. She did not want to be tuckered out before she even started the Grouse Grind, after all.

But her months of exploring the city had really toughened her up, and she was certain that she would have the stamina to achieve her goal.

When she reached the foot of the mountain she wandered around the tourist shop and ticket office, where a few tourists were buying tickets for the massive gondola to the top of the mountain.

Sumiko had read that you could hike up the Grouse Grind for free and then pay for the one-way gondola ride down after exploring the mountain top.

She then used the rest-room by the gift shop, so that she would not find herself half-way up the mountain needing to pee and have to go to the bathroom in the forest.

At the foot of the trail, Sumiko found a small stone pillar with some sort of electronic device installed in it. Curious, she watched as a few other hikers walked up and pressed some kind of electronic fobs against the pillar.

She had to know more. So when a couple arrived dressed more for an indoor workout than a mountain hike, with just a small fanny pack and a water bottle and no additional clothing approached the pillar, she asked: "Excuse me, what does this do?"

"It starts your time clock," said the man, without stopping, "and you check in again at the top to see your time. Bye!" He said, before he and his partner disappeared into the forest.

Not having a fob, Sumiko just made note of the time on her wristwatch and followed after them. She stopped to read a couple of warning sighs and the information billboard. She learned that the Grouse Grind has a vertical distance of 853 meters over almost 3 kilometers of trail, a 31% grade. The warning said that people without suitable clothing or with medical conditions are advised not to undertake such a strenuous trail, and that use is entirely at one's own risk.

This made sense to Sumiko after just a few hundred meters of hiking. The trail was so steep.

It was like climbing on Mother Nature's Stairmaster. The trail was very rough, with roots, stones and dirt making each step uneven and hazardous.

Now she understood why David had emphasized the need for rugged footwear. This observation was highlighted by the miserable faces on three Chinese women she met soon after. They were really struggling, coming down the mountain with sore feet and faces that showed utter panic.

Sumiko looked at their scuffed up and completely unsuitable pumps and wondered how could anybody be so stupid as to undertake such a hike without proper footwear.

Those were the only people she met who were headed down-hill. Everybody else was going up-hill.

Seeing the Chinese ladies suffering was one thing, but what Sumiko really found annoying were the mountain goats. That's what she called them to herself, those people who, like that first couple she had talked to at the trail head, were in such a hurry on their race against time that they impatiently pushed up from behind her and passed her on the way up the mountain. What's the big hurry? She thought to herself.

At one point, when she was about half way, Sumiko decided to get off the trail. In preparing for today, Sumiko had read about the trail. There had been nothing about the timing fobs but there had been lots of information about people leaving the trail and getting lost or injured. Just to play it safe, Sumiko did not go far from the trail, just 50 meters. She found a small side trail that took her out into an opening in the trees. There she found a flat log to sit on.

She looked around at her surroundings. There was a tall steel tower supporting wires. As she looked at it, trying to figure out what it was for, she heard the rumbling of wheels on wires and realized that it was a gondola tower. Suddenly the massive red and white gondola she had seen at the base of the mountain flew by, with the whirring sound coming to a climax right over her head.

Seconds later, an identical gondola whooshed down in the opposite direction, passing by on the other side of the tower. After having climbed about half way up the Grind so far, that gondola ride down now seemed like a great idea. But she had to press one up the hill, because she was only at the half way point.

As she got to her feet and walked along the short side-trail back to the steep up-hill snake of the main trail she remembered something her father used to joke with her about. He had very few English words but he had once been friends with an American who had complimented him on his stamina during a particularly ridiculous night of drinking at a Kyocera party, when her Papa had been young and reckless. The name stuck, and only came out when Papa faced a difficult or dreary task, requiring great stamina.

"Gambatte, Stamina-Man!" Sumiko said to herself, out loud, smiling.

On the final half-hour push to the top of the mountain, Sumiko caught up with three Japanese girls working their way up the hill slowly, stopping often but not quitting. In the few minutes of conversation that she had with them, Sumiko learned that they were also here on homestays. Predictably, they had taken to spending their days together on outings. Sumiko told them about the English – Japanese clubhouse on Alberni Street and encouraged them to make some English speaking friends.

Sumiko gave them a few encouraging words in Japanese and then carried on past them. They had been wearing sneakers, not ideal footwear, but not all that bad. But they were doing one thing that Sumiko really frowned upon, they were talking only in Japanese. They had clearly fallen into the trap of converting an ESL homestay into Japanese-only tourism. They would probably go home no farther ahead in terms of their English profiles than when they got off the plane.

Far better to treat Japanese friends in Vancouver like a fine wine. Nice to have some from time to time but not healthy to indulge in every day or all day long.

She knew that she was nearing the top of the Grouse Grind when she saw daylight shining on a large rock just above her. Sweating a bit at the intense effort to keep going on that last quarter of the trail, Sumiko had removed a few layers of clothing and was now down to a thin T-shirt and her khaki shorts. She felt strong and vigorous, without a care in the world or a worry on her mind. In fact, thought Sumiko, she had never felt more confident and alive.

Perhaps it was the exertion, or the somewhat Buddhist way she had been embracing life over the past few months. Or maybe it was just that at that moment, on her 25th birthday, Sumiko was in the prime of her life. She was living life the way it should be lived – to the fullest.

Feeling frisky and vigorous, she decided not to follow the trail around that last rock at the top of the Grouse Grind. It was only a few meters high, she figured, and there were a few lumps and crannies she could use for hand and foot-holds. She climbed up the rock face, not afraid that she could fall. It made her feel adventurous, even if there really wasn't any real danger.

And then she fell.

She did not fall off the rock face, she actually fell *into* a face. Because there, staring at her from the summit of her little rock, was the face that had lingered in her fantasies and dreams for the past six months. It was him. He was sitting right in front of her, looking at her in a relaxed manner that showed no hint of surprise.

"Hello, Sumiko! Nice to see you again, remember me?"

She was unable to speak or move. The love of her life, the man she had fallen in love with at first sight, the man who's name she did not even know, was talking to her – *and he knew her name*.

It was all she could do to sit down on the rock, less than a meter above where he was sitting, with his gear and his lunch laid out around him on the flat surface of boulder's summit.

"It is you!" was all she could say.

"Yes. And you!" he replied, his eyes drawing Sumiko deeply into his orbit, like a small moon captured by a larger planet.

"How? Where?" she stammered, settling herself to a more comfortable seated position. She could feel her heart racing, as much from the exertion of the climb up the rock face as from her emotions. She felt droplets of sweat trickling down from her armpits and from her forehead. A wave of excited confusion washed over her as she waited for him to take control of the conversation, hoping it would not turn out to be some terrible mistake or merely a dream.

"You are Sumiko Kichida, from Kyoto Japan, and you are the woman who has haunted my soul ever since I saw you in Yellowknife," he said.

"I? You?" Sumiko stopped breathing, waiting for more.

"When I got back to retrieve my sled from Beck's, you were already gone! I guess I should have said something to you but I was too nervous. So I went back to find you and introduce myself, find out who you were, but I was too late. When I got back there, you were long gone."

"You know my name?"

"Yeah, I got it from Beck. He thought that I had made an impression on you, but I was not so sure. So I wrote down your name and everything I could learn about you. I literally *interrogated* Beck for any clues he had about where you were from and where you were going. All he knew was that you had told him that you were from Kyoto and that you were on a homestay in Vancouver."

"And you came here? To find me?"

"Yes and no. I came here because this is my home. I once lived in Yellowknife, but for the last three years I've lived here, in Vancouver, in the West End. I was up in Yellowknife on a short-term contract with an engineering consulting firm. It was his sled that broke down."

"So how are the dogs?"

"Dogs?"

"Yes, the dogs from your sled," Sumiko said, a bit more relaxed, quickly growing comfortable in his presence.

"Dogsled? It was you who was on the dogsled that day. I was on a Skidoo."

"But I you called it a 'sled'," she said, confused.

"Yeah, a Skidoo is also called a sled, but a dogsled is not called a sled, it's called a dogsled," he explained with a smile.

"OK. But how did you find me, here today?"

"I found you by keeping my eye open for you everywhere I go, twenty-four hours a day, seven days a week. I've been asking every Japanese person I meet if they knew of a Sumiko Kichida from Kyoto. By the way, do you know how many Japanese girls there are in Vancouver?" he said. The way he shook his head and smiled as he spoke revealed just how desperately he had been searching for her.

"Finally, today, I decided to do the Grind and just hang around up here on Grouse. I was just sitting here having my lunch when I saw you working your way up the trail. With that baseball hat of yours blocking my view of your face, I was not sure it was you until your face came over the top of that rock! But then I recognized you immediately."

"And I recognized you too," Sumiko beamed, and paused for a moment, and then asked "but who are you? What is your name?"

"I'm Chris," he said, simply, "Chris McGee"

Blushing, "My name is Sumiko Kichida, but you know that!"

"Very pleased to meet make your acquaintance, Sumiko," said Chris, reaching out to take her small hand in his large, strong hand.

Feeling the rough coarseness and strength of his hand Sumiko gripped it as hard as she could, as though she wanted to hold on to him forever.

They sat there like that for several minutes, holding hands, not talking, but looking into each other's eyes in a state of equanimity.

They were both conscious of it, and both content to sit and hold hands. They could feel each other's heart-beats through their hands as the pulses found unison and became one single, strong rhythm.

Eventually, Sumiko broke the trance. She had been getting cold as her body cooled and the sweat began to give her chills. She wanted to change into her fresh T-shirt and put on a few layers of clothing.

"Well, Mr. Chris, what shall we do? I am getting cold, so can we go and find a place where I can change my clothes?" she said, letting go of his hand and getting up stiffly.

"Great idea. You brought a change of clothes? Very smart girl. You can change up there, in the Grouse Nest."

Walking up the staircase to the level where the lady's room was, with Chris in step behind her, Sumiko felt awkward at first. As stripped off her sweaty T-shirt in the washroom and put on a fresh one, Sumiko wondered if Chris would still be there when she came out. She wanted to rush out and see, or at least not make him wait, but something inside her told her to relax. It was as if she knew that she would be spending the rest of her life with him, and that there was no need to rush.

She took her time fixing up her make-up, which was minimal anyhow, and brushing her hair. She packed away her baseball cap, and let her hair hang freely to her shoulders. That's how she liked to look, how she felt most pretty, and how she wanted Chris to see her when she emerged from the bathroom.

He was not there when she got out! For a few terrifying minutes, Sumiko was heart-broken. She had been so sure that Chris was the real thing, that their meeting each other felt like the hand of destiny, that she had not even thought it possible that he would have gone.

Then Chris touched her shoulder, from behind.

Sumiko grabbed his hand in hers and spun around, as if she had caught some sort of elusive prey.

Then she saw the eager look in his eyes, she relaxed, and beamed a beautiful smile at him.

"I thought you gone! Where did you go?"

"You were really taking your time in there, Sumiko, so I went into the gift shop and bought you a present." He handed her a brown T-shirt, rolled up with a band of paper wrapped around it.

Sumiko opened it and read the writing on the T-Shirt: 'I Survived the Grouse Grind!'

"Thank you! I just love it. But I don't have a gift for you!"

"Yes, you do. Your gift to me is that you will spend the rest of the day with me!"

They spent the rest of the day hiking around on top of Grouse Mountain. They picked blueberries and huckleberries on the ski runs, admired the view of the city below, and took a lot of pictures. As they explored the alpine areas, they found out how much they had in common. They both loved nature and photography, they were both engineers, and they both wanted large families.

They did not kiss on that first date, even though it was obvious that they had fallen in love. There simply was no rush. Getting to know each other was more important than jumping into the more sensual side of love.

It was during dinner in the Eagle's Nest restaurant on top of the mountain, overlooking the most beautiful night skyline of the city below, that the moment happened.

Chris told Sumiko something that changed everything, and absolutely ruined her day.

"Sumiko. Before we go any further, there is something I must tell you."

She looked at him, blankly, and took a sip of her glass of wine, not expecting what would come next.

"There's no easy way to say this. I am married."

17

SELF RESCUE

The one place Sumiko felt she could get her mind off of Chris was Jericho Beach. All the way there, first on the bus down from Edgemont Village to the SeaBus terminal, then on the SeaBus to downtown, and the two busses it took to get across to the west side to Point Grey, Sumiko had felt like a zombie.

She had lost her spark. She took no joy out of the beautiful blue sky, the pleasant 24 degree day, or any of the other things that usually gave her pleasure.

She felt like an empty vessel.

Of course, she knew the reason why. She felt betrayed. Not only by Chris, for being married, but for herself, for having believed, even if just for a day, that her destiny could be so beautiful.

But it had felt so real, so genuine.

It was totally unacceptable to Sumiko, of course, this languishing in self pity. She had to do something to get her mind off of Chris, to get back to where she had been before going up the Grouse Grind.

So she decided to go windsurfing.

It was not as easy as she had thought. First, she had to convince the rather skeptical windsurfing instructor that she had enough experience to just rent a board and go out on her own. The tall blond boy, perhaps 18 years old, did not believe that she knew how to do a 'self rescue'.

The twenty knot wind was making choppy waves far too challenging conditions for beginners. But Sumiko was not a beginner. She had to convince the beach boy.

"I am actually very experienced," she insisted.

"Sorry, but if I rent you a board, and you get stuck out there amongst those freighters, I'll have to lock up here and come and get you with the rescue zodiac. Why don't you come back later, if the wind dies down?"

"What do I have to do to prove to you that I can handle these winds?"

"Well, can you show me a self- rescue?"

"You mean, what I will do if the conditions get too difficult for me, or if there is an equipment problem?" asked Sumiko.

"Yes. Can you demo that, here on the beach?"

"Sure. Which board can I use?"

"That 'One Design" over there." He said, pointing to a group of four or five boards, each with a sail leaned over on the board, the boom resting on the side rail of the windsurfing board.

The instructor was surprised to see that Sumiko could tell the difference between a Rocket-99, a Mistral, a Bic and a One-Design, as she walked right over to the correct board and grabbed the mast.

Smoothly swinging the sail on her hip so that it could flutter down-wind behind her, Sumiko walked backwards upwind until she found a clear space. She then walked back and tilted the windsurfing board onto its side, and removed the dagger board, dropping it onto her foot before releasing it gently to the sand.

She then hefted the large board and nosed it into the wind, and moved it to the clear space, just up-wind from the sail.

The instructor made a move to stop her from damaging the board, but Sumiko put it down correctly, so that it did not rest on the skeg. She then moved a small log over, to elevate the back end of the board, and flipped the board over. With the skeg now in the air over the sand, with no risk of being broken off, she was ready to go.

"Self rescue." she started. "Here I am out in the middle of the ocean. I am too tired to keep going, or there is an equipment failure. What will I do?"

Impressed so far, the instructor sat down on a log to watch the performance. A small group of other people gathered around to watch the petite Japanese girl give her demonstration.

Sumiko sat on the board, pretending to be sitting on a board floating in the water. She pulled the mast towards her, with the boom fluttering down wind.

"So I will do a self-rescue, to get back to the shore. First, I undo the out-haul, like this. Then I roll the sail inward, into the mast," she demonstrated, easily managing the sail flopping in the breeze. She kept good tension in the sail as she rolled it up, expertly gathering it in until it was rolled tight to the mast.

"Now I flip the boom out, and use the outhaul to tie the sail to the mast, in three places."

From the expert way she tied a series of half-hitches with the out-haul, it was obvious to everybody that she really knew her stuff.

"Now I use the up-haul to tie it some more, and the sail is now ready to go."

She then laid the sail along the board, and twisted her hips just enough to get the nicely packaged sail under her, on the board.

"Now, I lay on top of the sail, like this," Sumiko lay face-down on the board, "and paddle back in with my hands, Hawaii-Five-O style!"

The group of people cheered her demo, and the instructor walked up and reached a hand down to help Sumiko to her feet.

"That was the best 'Self Rescue' demonstration I have ever seen. Where did you learn to windsurf?

"In Japan, on Lake Biwako. It's a lot colder there, so I usually wore a dry suit. So now will you please rent me a board?"

"No," he smiled, "It's on the house!"

As Sumiko got dressed into a wetsuit and tried on different life jackets until she found one that fit her well, she realized that she had not been thinking of Chris.

To put him back out of her mind, she got busy moving her sail to the water's edge. With a flourish like casting a net, she tossed the sail into the water. Then she got the board and walked it down into the water, next to the sail.

After sliding the universal joint into the slot in the board, she was ready to go.

Before heading out, she took a moment to assess the conditions. The wind had died down a bit, to about fifteen knots from the west. A perfect cross-wind. With that, she knew, she could sail out and back, with no risk of being blown out to sea.

With a little effort, as she was standing a little too deep in the water, Sumiko used the Frisbee motion to draw the mast across the wind, generating some force on the sail. The sail flew up out of the water, and fluttered in a luff, directly down wind.

She then crossed hands, walking her grip onto the inner part of one side of the wishbone-style boom, and had her left hand close to the mast. Leaning the mast in close to her, she placed her left foot on the boar and gently nosed it into the right direction. She then simultaneously dipped the mast forward while reaching her right hand farther out on the boom, leaned back, and caught the wind in the sail.

She almost lost her balance as the force of wind in the sail pulled hard at her. She leaned back more, and pushed out with her legs, remembering to keep her knees bent.

With the force of the wind acting against the resistance of the dagger board, Sumiko's board shot outwards like a wet bar of soap between two hands. She soon whisked her way past the end of the pier, where some Asian men were crab-fishing, as usual. She looked around, but did not see any divers. Good, the Asian guys will get better crabs today, she thought.

It was the first time she had been windsurfing since her break up with Kenichi. Thinking about Kenichi helped keep her mind off of Chris.

She was a beautiful, kind, fun-loving and intelligent woman, she reminded herself. There would be no problem finding a lover who was not married.

While thinking about what it had been like to make love with Kenichi, which she had done in some rather unusual places, Sumiko lost track of where she was. She just kept going on her original tack, towards West Vancouver.

Soon she was in the middle of the bay, approaching one of the large cargo ships always at anchor off of Jericho Beach.

SNAP! And her sail pulled her off of her feet. She had not let go of the book fast enough, so she was catapulted several meters into the air.

SPLASH! And Sumiko was suddenly under water. When she came up for air, the sail was on top of her, keeping her from getting a breath of air.

Nearly in a panic, Sumiko held her breath and tried to figure out what to do. Her hands found the boom, and pulled the sail off of her.

The intake of life-giving air was quite a relief. But Sumiko was still very much in danger.

She looked behind her, and saw that the board was not far away.

She let go of the sail and swam towards the board.

The winds had picked up a bit, and the board was being blown farther out to sea, but Sumiko was a strong swimmer and she was actually swimming for her life, so she caught up to the board in a few minutes. She climbed on top of the board and straddled it with her legs, and tried to calm down.

As she sat there on her windsurfing board, with the wind and waves tossing her about, Sumiko felt that she was at the end of the line. She considered paddling over towards the sail, but decided that it was not worth wasting any energy to chase the sail. She knew that she was still in danger, and that the smart thing to do was focus on saving herself, and not the equipment.

She looked around, trying to figure out where she was. Everything looked different from where she now was. So she used the back of her right hand, to remind herself where everything was supposed to be. That really helped, as she oriented herself. With the north shore mountains behind her, downtown to her left, and the open ocean to her right, Jericho Beach had to be right in front of her.

Squinting as she looked up-sun towards the south, Sumiko made out the Jericho Beach Sailing Centre. It looked really small.

She realized that she was a long way from safety, and lay down and began to paddle.

She was no longer afraid, as she had taken action and was doing something to save herself. She also felt a great surge of self-confidence. She knew that her knowledge of the local geography, and her decision to abandon the sail, were a few of the factors working in her favor.

But she was still a bit afraid, which kept her motivated to paddle hard.

Brian, the instructor at Windsure Windsurfing, did not see that Sumiko was in any trouble until he saw her paddle around the end of the pier and come into view.

He walked down to the edge of the water to greet her.

"Are you ok? What happened to the sail?"

Out of breath but feeling the exhilaration one gets after avoiding death, Sumiko caught her breath before explaining.

"The universal joint broke. I was too far out, so I left the sail behind. Sorry!"

"Don't worry about that, it's insured. I'm just glad you made it back alright," he said.

Just then, a catamaran sailboat zoomed in towards the shore with the sail.

"Hey, Brian, is this one of yours?"

"Yeah! Thanks, Ted."

"We couldn't find who it belonged to. Should we alert the Search and Rescue folks?"

"No. There's no need for SAR. She self-rescued. She's right here, she's OK."

Thirty minutes later, Sumiko was having a much needed cheeseburger and fries in the outdoor canteen on the second floor of the Sailing Center, with Brian and a few others from Windsure Windsurfing.

"That was really something, Sue," Brian said, "were you scared?"

"Oh yeah, I was scared without poop!"

"You mean 'scared shitless', right?"

"Yeah, that's it, scared shitless!" Sumiko laughed. "But it sure helped me forget about my problems!"

"I know what you mean. I had a similar experience myself last fall. I was on a short-board doing some wave-jumping, when my harness failed. The winds were too strong. We never found my high-clue sail!" said Brian.

"What problems?" asked Brian's girlfriend, Mary.

"Oh, I don't want to get into it."

"Oh yeah, I know. It's a man, isn't it?" Mary said to Sumiko.

"How did you know?"

"I know that look. He broke your heart?"

"Yes."

"How long had you been together?"

Sumiko thought for a moment. "Maybe six hours."

"Six hours? And he broke your heart?"

"Well, it's complicated."

"Go on, it sounds interesting."

"We met six months ago, in Yellowknife. But we did not know each other's names or how to contact each other. Then I suddenly found him on Grouse Mountain, when I did the Grouse Grind last week."

"You found a guy you had only met once, six months ago? What was it, 'love at first sight'?"

"You could say that. We had a wonderful day walking in the alpine areas on Grouse Mountain. Then we had a romantic dinner in the Eagle's Nest restaurant." Sumiko told the story as if it was a hundred years ago. Retelling the story brought back strong feelings, but for some reason Sumiko felt comfortable with these beach bums.

"Sounds very romantic so far. Six hours, eh? What went wrong?"

"Just when I felt that we were both ready to say 'I love you', which should be impossible for a first day together, he destroyed the moment by telling me that he was married." Sumiko was suddenly very emotional, and hid her face behind her hands, trying to hide her tears.

"What a bastard. How dare he be married! What a cheating bastard! Did he have any explanation?"

"I don't know. I spit out my wine all over the table and then I threw up in the bathroom! Then I ran away, and got on the gondola, without looking back. You should have seen how ugly I looked by the time I got home, I was such a mess!" Even with tears in her eyes, Sumiko also had to laugh at that. So did Brian and his girlfriend.

"Right on, girl. Too bad you didn't puke all over him!" said Mary.

"Well, I did get wine all over his shirt!"

They all broke out laughing, and somehow Sumiko was starting to feel a lot better. Perhaps it had something to do with having had her life in danger just hours before. Now, a romance gone sour did not feel like the end of the world anymore.

"He did try to say that he was separate from his wife. As if that makes a difference. Of course he is separate, he is a different person."

"What do you mean?" asked Brian.

"As I ran away from the restaurant, he kept saying that he was separate from his wife for eleven months."

"That's good news."

"How is that good news? Of course he is separate, if he is not in love then they are not unity, and he is cheating his wife. Or he was hoping to cheat her, with me!" said Sumiko, indignant.

"Sumiko, so do you know what 'separated' means?"

"I think so. It means not union."

"But in the context of a marriage?"

"I'm not sure I know what you are saying."

"Sumiko, it means that he and his wife are going to be divorced."

Skeptical, Sumiko asked: "If that was true, then why didn't he get divorced?

"Sumiko, how do people get a divorce in Japan?"

"It is easy. You just go to the local prefecture office and fill out some forms, and 48 hours later, you are divorced! Of course, there are always legal issues like custody of children, property, and things like that. My aunt, Honoko, went through it all when she caught her chikan of a salaryman boyfriend cheating on her. Why, is it different here in Canada?

"Wow! Is it really that easy in Japan?"

"Yes."

"Well, it is a lot different here, I can tell you from personal experience. Even if you get along, it takes over a year. You have to be legally separated for a year, first of all," said Mary.

Sumiko was silent for a minute, trying to work it all out in her mind.

"Do you mean that Chris was living with his wife, separated, for a year?"

"No. Probably not. You see, when a married couple get separated, they have to stop living together. The idea is that the courts want to be sure that they took some time, at least a year, to try to work things out, to reconcile, before a divorce can be approved by the courts."

"That's very strange," said Sumiko. "You mean they have to prove that they really, really don't want to be married anymore? That's not fair, it's like they are trapped in the marriage!" said Sumiko.

"Well, that is how it is. Marriage is supposed to be a life-long commitment, after all."

"I guess." Sumiko said, looking upset.

"So, kitten, it could mean that your man is truly free and clear. With what, eleven months of separation behind him? That means he can have a divorce in a month. So he's fair game, as long as he is not tied up emotionally. Why did their marriage fail, anyhow?"

"I have no idea. I puked and ran away when I learned he was married!"

"You haven't talked to him on the phone since then?"

"No. I don't know his number."

From the pale, detached look that had come over Sumiko's face, Mary knew what was going on behind those pretty little brown eyes.

Sumiko. I think you have made a terrible mistake, haven't you?" she said, gently.

"Yes, I think I have…"

"Can you find him? What do you know about him?

Slowly, as if there was no point in it, Sumiko began. "His name is Chris McGee.

"Where does he live, in the city?"

"Yes. He said that he lives in the West End."

Mary got up and retrieved the phone book from inside the café. Two minutes later, she was dialing a number into her cell phone.

Sumiko held her breath, terrified. She could hear the sound of the phone ringing.

"Hello." It was him.

"Are you heart-broken?" asked Mary, without even telling him who she was.

"Excuse me! Who is this?"

"Are you in love with someone, yes or no?"

"Who is this? Are you talking about Sumiko?" Sumiko could hear urgency in Chris's voice, even some pain.

"I am a friend of hers. She's sitting right here beside me. You have one chance to explain yourself to me, or I hang up. Are you single, happily married, divorced, or separated. What is your status?"

"I am getting a divorce next month. I was married a year ago in Las Vegas. It was all a big mistake, and I haven't seen her since our wedding night. We have nothing to do with each other, other than having been tied up in our misadventure. It means nothing, and I am single. Please let me talk to Sumiko, let me try to explain." he said, sounding sincerely anguished.

"Sumiko, it's for you." Mary and Brian discretely moved to another table, giving Sumiko some privacy.

From what they could see, Sumiko and Chris were having an important conversation, but it seemed to be going well.

After a few minutes, Mary noticed Sumiko desperately digging through her purse until she found a pen and a notebook. She furiously wrote in her notebook, and then fumbled with the phone, trying to figure out how to hang up and turn it off.

Two hours later, after Brian and Mary let Sumiko off in front of Chris's apartment, there was an impressive looking man standing at the road-side waiting for Sumiko, and they drove off.

Sumiko's budding romance was back on track.

18

JUST DO IT!

Just a few months after resuming their romance, Sumiko and Chris were cuddling in the love seat in Sumiko's suite in Edgemont Village, watching the movie, Titanic, together.

After the movie they talked about how life can be so adventurous, if only one has the courage to take a few risks and follow your heart.

"You are absolutely right, Sumichan. After all, it's what brought us together."

"So let's go on an adventure someplace!"

"Like where?" asked Chris.

"I don't know why, but somehow I got the idea that it would be fun to cycle across Australia!"

"Really? That's very ambitious Sumichan. What do you know about Australia?"

"Not much. I know it is hot there, and that it was once an English colony."

"But what about your English classes out at UBC, and your volunteering at the Japan-Canada Friendship House?" asked Chris.

"I can afford to miss two weeks, and I can afford the tickets. What better time to go on an impromptu adventure than now. We'd be together for every minute. It would be the two of us against the world! – like in Titanic!" Sumiko said enthusiastically.

"What places in Australia would you like to see?"

"I want to visit the Barossa Valley!" said Sumiko.

"Why?"

"I have an open invitation to visit a vineyard," Sumiko said with a smile.

Two weeks later, they arrived in Sydney. It took them two weeks to cycle the fourteen hundred kilometers to Adelaide. Each day they would cycle about one hundred kilometers, stopping to explore the towns and spots of interest along the way.

There had been a few difficult days, as they encountered severe headwinds on many days. From Sumiko's perspective, the challenge was well worth the effort. It tested her theory that the true test of a couple is how they handled adversity. If they overcome it by working together, not turning on each other, then they had a good chance of success in marriage.

And marriage was on her mind, even though she and Chris had not discussed it yet.

When they pulled into the hilly neighborhood on the west side of Adelaide, where they were going to stay with some cycling contacts they had made on the internet, Sumiko was in for a surprise.

They recognized the retired couple, their hosts for their arrival day, from their website.

"You must be Sheila and Bruce?" Asked Chris.

"Very funny, Canuck! Yes, we are Sandra and Bill. But you're right, I'm the Sheila and he's the Bruce." laughed the old lady. Welcome to our flop house! You are the Canadians, right? We're also expecting a pair of cyclists from America."

"Thanks, Yes, I am Chris, and this is my fiancée, Sumiko."

Sumiko broke out in tears of joy, and looked at Chris.

He was down on his knees, reaching up to her with a diamond ring in his hands. Sumiko had no idea that he was going to propose, nor any suspicions that he was going to do it on this trip. But it felt absolutely perfect that, after reaching their goal of riding that last one hundred and fifty kilometers over challenging, hilly terrain, without losing the fun or backing from the challenge, and Sumiko felt that it was the perfect time to decide their future.

"Will you marry me, Sumichan," said Chris, looking absolutely certain that she would say yes.

"Yes, I will!" said Sumiko.

Later that night, when Sumiko called her family to announce the news, there was yet another surprise in store for her.

Her father informed her that Chris had written to him in Japanese, asking for Mr. Kichida's permission for Chris to propose to Sumiko. Her father had agreed, impressed that the young man had shown enough respect to ask, and agreed to keep it secret until Chris had proposed.

The next day, when Sumiko and Chris cycled up to the Barossa Valley to stay with the Clarke's, Sumiko was giddy with excitement as she introduced her Fiancée, Chris, to Jocko and Andrea.

The Clarkes were wonderful hosts, giving Sumiko and Chris their own little cabin to stay in, down by a lazy old river at the far end of the vineyard, where Jocko's grandfather had first stared Thistle & Clarke wineries.

Chris and Sumiko began to plan their wedding right then and there, having already selected a range of fine wines from Jocko diverse range of wines.

And, of course, the Clarkes were at the top of the guest list!

19

WHEN NOT TO JUMP

The young couple had announced their engagement and even set the date for their upcoming wedding, and then began to give serious attention to planning for the future.

Many of their conversations took place as they enjoyed long walks in many places they loved to go in the greater Vancouver area. The conversation about how many children they wanted took place on the Baden Powell trail, starting at the Mount Seymour road and ending close to Horseshoe Bay. They were too tired to hike all the way back to where they had parked Chris's Jeep Cherokee, so they had taken a taxi back.

They were in agreement that they would have a few children before deciding how many they would plan for, but they both wanted lots of noisy kids.

The conversation about where they wanted to live had taken place on a walk around the Sea Wall around Stanley Park. And their conversation about when and how to take care of Sumikos' immigration status had taken place on their wonderful misadventure in the Pacific Spirit Park. They had gotten completely lost in the large forest park out on Sumiko's middle finger, near the University Of British Columbia. They had come out of the trails at the ocean, in an unfamiliar place.

Chris noticed the smell of something unusual burning, and teased Sumiko.

"Sumichan. Can you smell something in the air?"

"Yes. It smells like wet leaves burning. What is it"

"It's some hippies dippies getting high."

"What's a hippie? And what's getting high?"

"A hippie is someone with long hair, who cares deeply about the planet. So deeply that they typically live in tents in the forest, under bridges or in abandoned houses. They share love and drugs with each other, and tend to be rather dirty." Chris said, jokingly.

"You mean homeless people?"

"Not exactly. The hippie generation was famous in California in the 1960s. You know, free love and pass the pot."

"Pot? For food?"

"No, pot to smoke Marijuana. Getting high."

"Oh, I understand. I have seen some 'dippies' at the youth hostel."

"Hippies. Yeah, that's where you find them today. Shh!" Chris said, as they approached a group of hippies sitting in a nook made by a few large logs washed up on the shoreline. They had made something of a camp site, with a small fire burning and some bread roasting on sticks near the flames. A baby was crawling around naked in the sand, while a toddler, also naked, was poking a stick into the abandoned carcass of a crab.

Sumiko looked up from the fire and children, to get a quick look at the adults.

There were three men and two young women. One of the women was wearing a beautiful stitch of fabric around her waist, like a sarong. One of the men was wearing a colorful knitted toque, with bright orange, red, and yellow colors. Some of his hair was escaping from the tuque, in long pony tails that Sumiko knew were called 'dreadlocks'.

Other than the sarong and the one toque, there was no other clothing.

Sumiko was embarrassed when she caught herself staring at one of the men's 'hardware', and pulled her glance away from the well-hung man.

"Hello! Want to join us? We've got lots of BC Bud, if you want some!" said the man who's 'package' Sumiko had been staring at.

"No thanks!" said Chris, smiling. Sumiko could tell that his gaze had lingered on the young women, one of whom Sumiko noticed had very large breasts.

After they had walked far enough away from the hippies, and Sumiko could no longer smell the marijuana in the air, she realized something.

"Hey! This must be Wreck Beach!"

"You're right, Sumiko, it must be. I'm surprised I did not realize it before, but we are at the end of the west side. I think if we keep going another few hundred meters, we'll find the Gun Towers."

"What are the Gun Towers?"

"They are concrete towers that once held huge guns. They were abandoned after the war, and that's why this beach is called 'Wreck Beach'. So do you want to go topless?"

"No way!" replied Sumiko, aghast.

After they found one of the Gun Towers, Sumiko and Chris followed a trail that led up from the beach to the University of British Columbia.

They were suddenly back in civilization, with modern facilities and dormitories of the university all around.

They walked on for a while, looking for a bus stop or a map, so they could figure out how to find their way back to where Chris had parked his Jeep at the head of Salish Trail, in the Pacific Spirit Forest Park.

They soon found themselves at a bus stop, and began to wait for the bus, until Chris noticed that they were right in front of the Museum of Anthropology.

It was just another example of the way that Sumiko and Chris spent their time together. They would set out on some plan for a long walk, and find unexpected little adventures and interesting things to explore.

They spent the rest of the day exploring the main exhibits in the fabulous museum. Sumiko was impressed with the First Nations exhibits, such as totem poles, cedar boxes, and long boats.

Later that night, while Sumiko and Chris made love, there was a little extra excitement for Sumiko. She had not intended to, but thinking about the nudists at Wreck Beach made her wonder if there would be a time and a place where she and Chris could go nude.

After they were done, she mentioned it to Chris. She was a little shy to bring it up, but so far Sumiko had found that she could talk to Chris about anything, even more sensual or personal things than she could have confided with Keiko, her best friend back in Japan.

"Chris, are there some beaches we could camp on, where there are no other people?"

"Sure. Why? Thinking about what I'm thinking about?" Chris said, rolling to his side to look at Sumiko.

As he caressed her naked thigh with his strong hands, she closed her eyes and listened to him.

"There are lots of great beaches to camp at, some are on the Sunshine Coast, where you went with the Goodwins last winter."

"You mean Sechelt and Gibsons? But it was so rocky on those beaches."

"There are more, that most people don't know about. You have to know the logging roads to find some of them. Or you can take a small boat to some isolated little islands that have small sandy beaches. Absolute privacy, if you want to go skinny dipping."

"What's skinny dipping?"

"It's when you swim in your birthday suit."

"Birthday suit?"

"You know, what were you wearing when you were born?"

"Nothing. I was….oh!"

"But the best place to go camping is on Vancouver Island. There are waterfalls, lakes, forests, mountains, and great beaches. Some are so remote that you have to hike 50 kilometers to see them, like the West Coast Trail. Others are shorter hikes, like Capt Scott, but you have to drive all the way to the northwest end of the Island to get to the trail head. And there are lots of little beaches you can drive to, but they are not as private. The best of these is Long Beach, out near Tofino."

"Wow, I had no idea there were so many beaches and places to explore."

"Sumiko, if you really like camping, I mean really hiking with everything you need on your back, then you're talking to the right fiancé!"

"So I don't have to go find another one?" Sumiko teased.

When Chris told her how the pounding surf and the gentle wind action in the trees makes one feel so relaxed and at peace in nature, when camping near the ocean, it reminded Sumiko of some of their nights camping by their bicycles when they were on their bike trip in Australia.

It made them both interested in making love again.

When Sumiko saw that hungry, eager look in her lover's eyes, just an hour after he had climaxed with her so satisfyingly, she doubted that he could possibly do the job so soon again.

His gentle touches and firm pressures in just the right places soon brought Sumiko to the summit, where he held her in a finely tuned balance between the uninhibited release of orgasm and the constant upward spiraling of sensual energy.

She had never been so aroused by any man, and when he finally pushed her over the top, the climax was quite simply mind-blowing. She let go completely and found herself flying high in a universe of sensations that, even as she came down from it, were a pleasant return to earth that somehow reminded her of the sento-glow.

They fell asleep in each other's arms and later woke up in the same position, facing each other.

Two weeks after their walk at Wreck Beach, Sumiko and Chris drove to the United States of America.

This short trip really made Sumiko nervous. They had decided that they would leave Canada so that Sumiko could apply for Landed Immigrant Status in Canada. Chris had explained to Sumiko that they really only had two good options.

Their first option was for Sumiko to marry Chris, and then apply for Landed Immigrant Status as Family Class – Spouse. But that would mean waiting several months, and then any time she spent away from Canada would delay her citizenship. So the other option was to apply based on her being Chris's fiancée.

They had heard from other Japanese-Canadian couples that it would be easier for Sumiko to "jump the lines" by simply staying in Canada and applying in Canada. This is against the rules, because she was in Canada on a student visitor visa, so according to the rules she must leave Canada and apply for a new immigration status from outside of Canada. While there was some attraction in the convenience of simply staying in Canada and "jumping the line", there were also some risks. For example, if she did that, then if she had to leave Canada at any time to visit Japan, then she could be denied re-entry and have to re-apply. Sumiko did not want to cheat the system, and did not want to become a hostage to the immigration rules.

By going to Seattle to apply, even if it made her feel uncomfortable at the very slim possibility that it would be rejected, Sumiko was certain that she was doing the right thing. But she was also upset to learn that in Canada, people who cheat the system are often rewarded with getting their citizenship faster or more conveniently.

In any case, Sumiko had decided that this was one of those circumstances and it was best not to jump.

Chris and Sumiko had a great day in Seattle. After dropping off their application at the Canadian Consulate in Seattle, they spent the day downtown and at Pike Place Fish market, where Japanese – American fishermen entertained them by throwing huge salmon into the air and catching them in News Paper, while shouting in Japanese: "Heyyyy – Yaaa" It reminded Sumiko of home. Her other home.

On their way home, Sumiko enjoyed a few hours finishing reading a book on her Kindle Fire. Just as she was about to start another book, they reached the US side of the Canada-USA border. They stopped at the International Peace Gardens. There was a special small garden called: 'Japanese Garden Bridge', that really made Sumiko feel homesick.

The more that Sumiko made Vancouver her home, and the more excited she was about getting married and exploring life and love with her man, the more Sumiko began to wonder how bad the homesickness would become.

It was not enough to make her have any doubts, but it was a concern.

It was the only topic that she was afraid to bring up with Chris. Little did she know that it would become a very serious issue for them in the not too distant future.

20

GIVING A DAUGHTER AWAY

Mr. Kichida was nervous. He was not sure that he was being driven to the right place. Thank goodness for Aikochan and her excellent English skills, he thought, as the taxi made its way towards Brock House.

They had only had one hour to change at the hotel before getting into the taxi. The driver appeared to be from Pakistan or India, and did not seem to understand English very well. Aiko clearly told him the address, and he began to drive, but did not say anything to the Kichida's to indicate that he knew where he was going. To make matters worse, he was talking in some strange language as he drove, using a 'hands-free' device, so it looked as if he was ranting to the Kichidas in a crazy language that they did not understand.

He tried to relax, telling himself that he would get to the right place and be in time, but when he stopped worrying about the taxi, he began to worry about having to say goodbye to his baby girl, giving her away to a man he had not met.

His role in the ceremony had been explained to him, but it still seemed strange to him, quite different from how such thing are done in Japan.

After entering the building, Mr. Kichida was met by a very large man with a grey beard.

"Are you Mr. Kichida?" he asked, only to stare into the blank faces of the Kichida family. So he tried again, this time in what little Japanese he had learned in the short time he had to prepare for the event.

"Anatatachi wa, Kichida desu ka?"

"Hai. Yes, we Kichida. Who you?"

"I'm Mr. McGee, Chris's father. It is a pleasure to meet you at last, Kichida San! Chris and Sumiko will be so relieved to hear that you made it in time. So are you ready to give your daughter away?" laughed the big man.

"Yes. Please help me. My English terrible." said Mr. Kichida. But as much as he was ashamed at not having learned more English, he was deeply honoured that Mr. McGee was learning some Japanese. It made him feel more comfortable, that his daughter was joining an honourable family, and that there would be some liaison between the two families. This strange looking giant of a man, Chris's father, seemed to be a good man, a man that Mr. Kichida could find a way to communicate with.

"You'll do fine. I was just as nervous as you are when I gave away Chris's sister, Julia, when she got married last year!"

"Can you take us at Sumiko?"

"Sure! I'll take you to Sumiko. She's with the ladies, up in the dressing room. Come this way, she's been asking for you constantly," he said as he led the excited family up to see the bride.

Hours later, after all the formalities and speeches had been completed, even Mrs. Kichida was having fun. There were lots of other family members and other guests from Japan who had arrived days before the Kichidas. Several of Sumiko's university friends were there, and even Atsuko's nasty sister, Honoko, had come out.

With Chris and Sumiko speaking both English and Japanese, along with a few other bilingual

Japanese – Canadian guests, there were enough cross-cultural connections at every table so that all the wedding guests were able to communicate. That somehow made the entire wedding that much more special, people from opposites sides of the world were getting along famously.

When Sumiko arrived on the dance floor dressed in more casual clothes, it was the third change of costume for the bride in less than ten hours. First, she had been dressed in a traditional Japanese Kimono, for the pre-wedding photo-shoot by the elegant arched bridge in Jericho Park, adjacent to Brock House. Then she had changed into a beautiful bridal gown, shining bright white in the afternoon sunshine out on the lawn where the ceremony took place. Finally, after the ceremony, the speeches, the dinner and the wedding cake portion of the evening were completed, the dancing had begun with a waltz performed by the bride and groom.

Soon after that Sumiko had snuck up to the dressing room to change out of her bridal dress and into a comfortable yet elegant dress and comfortable dancing shoes. She spent the next two hours straight dancing, and getting everybody else to dance. Everybody had a lot of fun.

At one point, while Sumiko was dancing with three of her girlfriends from Japan, Sumiko suddenly stopped and stared at the best man,

Derek Osborne. He was embracing a beautiful woman with light brown hair.

"Wait a minute. Who exactly is that woman in Derek's arms? – He did not bring a date!" Sumiko McGee asked her fresh new husband.

"I don't know. I think she said her name is Susan or Sharon or something. I thought she was a friend of yours."

"No, I've never seen her before in my life."

As Sumiko and Chris admired the romantic embrace of Sharon and Derek, Sumiko looked around for the seating plan. It had been pushed off to the side of the room. She led Chris over to it and looked at the names. Then she found Sharon's name hand-written on one of the spare tags. It had been placed at the table with their Australian friends, Jocko and Andrea Clarke, and the Goodwin kids.

"Chris! Sharon was not on the guest list, so unless she came with Derek, I think she crashed our wedding!" Sumiko said, smiling with admiration as she thought about it.

"Do you want me to call security, and have her removed?" asked Chris.

"Are you kidding? This is a riot! Imagine the story they'll have to tell their kids! "

"What do you mean? Do you really think they'll end up getting married?"

"Oh yeah, Chris, I am absolutely certain. Not only because of the way they are looking at each other, but also because I just happen to know this one important thing: romances that get their start in an unexpected adventure always wind up in a successful marriage," Sumiko said, as Chris took her in his arms and kissed her with gusto.

The guests noticed as Chris arched Sumiko's back and leaned her head over heels, kissing her like it was a tango dance. Everybody cheered, and even Derek and Sharon took a break from their own making out, to cheer.

Minutes later, with their own passions rising, the newlyweds looked into each other's eyes, silently communicating that it was time. Chris gave the signal to the limousine driver who had been standing by just out of sight, to prepare the car.

"Let's get out of here, my love, and let the honeymoon begin!"

The wedding guests were soon herded out to the steps leading down to the private driveway, and Sumiko and her husband had both changed back into tux wedding dress, just to make the exit that much more enjoyable.

The culminating event of the wedding was still to occur. People seemed to know it was coming, and began to gather around. Sumiko put one foot up on a chair as Chris knelt down in front of it. When Chris removed the sexy garter band from Sumiko's leg many of the more conservative Japanese women look shocked but the Japanese men applauded loudly. The Japanese women smiled politely at first, not sure if they really should get involved, and then started to get into the spirit of the tradition, and cheered as well.

When Sumiko threw the bouquet over her shoulder, it was caught by Sharon, the mystery woman, who looked nervously at the man she just met, and fallen in love with.

As Mr. and Mrs. McGee rushed under the upraised and clasped hands of two rows of guests, other guest threw rice and confetti into the air, and suddenly Sumiko and Chris were making their escape, climbing into the waiting limousine.

As the elegant car began to drive away on Point Grey Road, streamers attached to the bumper began blowing in the wind: 'Just Married'.

Thirty six hours later, after spending the entire night, next day and following night in the Honeymoon Suite at the Bayshore Inn Hotel, right next to Stanley Park, they took a taxi to the airport for their two week honeymoon in Scotland.

They would not be staying at a hotel, as they had been given an early wedding gift from Jocko Clarke. He had arranged for the McGees to spend their wedding in the Clarke family's hereditary estate, owned and operated by his brother, William. And it was in the same region of Scotland as the McGee family originated, so it was a perfect place to have a honeymoon and explore a part of her husband's Scottish heritage.

The only open question that the young married couple was whether or not Chris should accept the unexpected job offer he had received from the Omron corporation, for a research position at their facility not far from Lake Biwako.

Sumiko had been gentle in persuading Chris that accepting the offer for the three year job was the right thing for him to do.

She did not at that time inform Chris that she was already pregnant, and wanted her first child to be born in Japan. She was saving that for another time.

The wedding had been enough excitement for one day.

終わり

The End

BOOK COUPONS

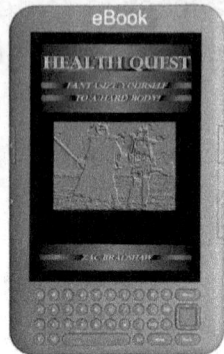

$3.50 off **Winter Kill** – *War With China Has Already Begun:* www.createspace.com/3537111 enter code PAC6SETA

$2.50 off **Homestay** – *A Japanese Girl's Romantic ESL Adventure In Vancouver,* Canada: www.createspace.com/ 3715916 enter code 9JGPMV3B

$2.00 off **Health Quest** – *Fantasize Yourself to a Hard Body* www.createspace.com/3625224

For additional discount codes, participate in the Rewards Program at www.fleacircusbooks.com

SEARCH FOR "GENE SKELLIG" AT AMAZON.COM

ABOUT THE AUTHOR

Currently serving as an Air Force pilot, Gene was inspired to write *Homestay* by his many positive experiences teaching English in Kyoto, Japan, with Osaka-based Overseas Training Center (OTC). Gene has studied an eclectic range of subjects, and has a degree in Philosophy from the University of British Columbia in his home town of Vancouver. Gene is also a founding member of Flea Circus Books. To find out more about Gene, explore his page through FleaCircusBooks.com.

ENHANCED SELF-PUBLISHING

This book was published through a new paradigm in publishing. Flea Circus Books. This royalties-based collaborative system provides authors, content collaborators, subject matter experts, illustrators, cover artists and niche marketing entrepreneurs with an ethical, predator-free interchange. With a break-even point on the order of just a few dozen books due to the low cost structure FCB permits, new authors like myself are able to set realistic and attainable goals.

- Get involved at: **www.fleacircusbooks.com** -

www.ingramcontent.com/pod-product-compliance
Lightning Source LLC
LaVergne TN
LVHW051500080426
835509LV00017B/1849